SO-AZY-621

"*How Leaders Decide* is an engaging, highly snackable read. From William McKnight's 'codifying curiosity' at 3M, to Henri Dunant's founding of the International Red Cross, to Henry Ford's decision to double the pay of his factory workers, the book is rich in examples that celebrate ethical judgment and action, not the pursuit of personal profit or shareholder return."

—*Mike O'Toole, President at PJA Advertising and Marketing, coauthor of* The Unconventionals

"For busy executives who appreciate the power of brevity, insight, and pragmatism, these fifty-two historical gems served up by Greg Bustin hit the bull's eye. Leaders willing to invest a few minutes of time each week can draw inspiration from these dramatic events to bolster their own experience and confidence when it's time to make their next significant decision."

—*Ashley Sheetz, Chief Marketing Officer, At Home Group Inc.*

"Talk about the perfect combination! In *How Leaders Decide*, popular management coach Greg Bustin combines fascinating history with succinct leadership insights to showcase fifty-two of the greatest leadership decisions the world has seen. Whether we're hurtling through space with the ill-fated *Apollo 13* astronauts, gazing across the river Rubicon with Julius Caesar, or watching Steve Jobs rescue Apple from insolvency, we are learning from momentous decisions made by proven leaders. *How Leaders Decide* is designed to provide a decision lesson for each week of the year, but readers should not be surprised if they find themselves rushing through its compelling lessons the first day."

—*Gordon Leidner, author of* The Leadership Secrets of Hamilton

"Greg's fast-paced, insightful stories about history's greatest triumphs and tragedies are punctuated with provocative questions that invite leaders to pause, reflect, and then apply these lessons in their own world. Though I was familiar with many of the events Greg examines, I thoroughly enjoyed learning more about the story-behind-the-story of these history-shaping decisions. I also appreciated the connection Greg makes between the stories of yesterday and leadership today. This is a great read with powerful takeaways."

—*Ray Napolitan, Executive Vice President, Nucor*

"Through fifty-two inspiring and instructional vignettes, Bustin's unique vantage point—which exposes him to hundreds of contemporary leaders at the top of their game—creates a book of true long-term value. *How Leaders Decide* focuses on brilliant and bungling decisions from history while prompting incisive questions for your own organization right now. How can you not love a book that demands only ten minutes a week but gives back so much food for thought?"

—*Hugh Kennedy, EVP Planning, partner at PJA Advertising and Marketing, coauthor of* The Unconventionals

Also by Greg Bustin

Take Charge!
Lead the Way
That's a Great Question
Accountability: The Key to Driving a High-Performance Culture

Visit bustin.com for tools and exercises and
to subscribe to receive free content.

HOW LEADERS DECIDE

A Timeless Guide to

Making Tough Choices

GREG BUSTIN

Published by Sourcebooks, Inc.
P.O. Box 4410, Naperville, Illinois 60567-4410
(630) 961-3900
Fax: (630) 961-2168
sourcebooks.com

Library of Congress Cataloging-in-Publication Data

Names: Bustin, Greg.
Title: How leaders decide : history's most unique, momentous, unusual, and courageous decisions / Greg Bustin.
Description: Naperville, Illinois : Sourcebooks, [2018] | Includes bibliographical references and index.
Identifiers: LCCN 2018023558 | (hardcover : alk. paper)
Subjects: LCSH: Leadership—History—Case studies. | Decision-making—History—Case studies.
Classification: LCC HM1261 .B887 2018 | DDC 303.3/409—dc23 LC record available at https://lccn.loc.gov/2018023558

Printed and bound in the United States of America.
MA 10 9 8 7 6 5 4 3 2 1

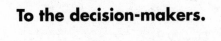

To the decision-makers.

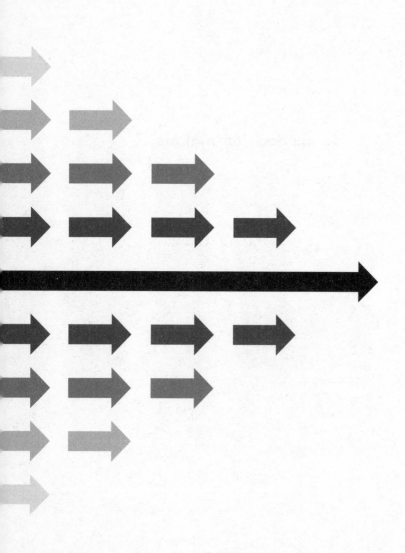

Table of Contents

PREFACE   xix
INTRODUCTION   xxv

WEEK 1
Bruce Ismay Reviews the Designs of *Titanic*   1

WEEK 2
Alfred Nobel Reimagines His Legacy   6

WEEK 3
Julius Caesar Crosses the Rubicon   11

WEEK 4
A Letter Triggers William McKnight's Curiosity
and Launches an Empire   16

WEEK 5
Liddy, Mitchell, Dean, and Magruder Plan
the Watergate Break-In   21

WEEK 6
Queen Elizabeth Declines to Marry, Producing
No Heir to the Throne   26

WEEK 7
Reich Minister Speer Counters Hitler's Plan
to Destroy Germany's Art and Infrastructure   31

WEEK 8
Pope Gregory XIII Issues Papal Bull Reforming
the Julian Calendar   36

WEEK 9
Henri Dunant Forms the International Red Cross   41

WEEK 10
Colonel William B. Travis Gives His Alamo
Defenders a Choice: Leave, or Stay and Die   46

WEEK 11
Franklin D. Roosevelt's "Hundred Days"
Combats the Great Depression   51

WEEK 12
John Adams Agrees to Defend British Soldiers
Charged with Murder   56

WEEK 13
Abraham Lincoln's Shrewd Idea Exposes the South
as the Aggressor   61

WEEK 14
The Final Days of America's Bloodiest Conflict
Teach Us about Loss   66

WEEK 15
Apollo 13's Mid-Flight Explosion Threatens
Crew's Safe Return to Earth   71

WEEK 16
Winston Churchill Gives the Worst Speech
of His Life   76

WEEK 17
Barack Obama Deploys SEAL Team 6 on Operation
Neptune Spear   81

WEEK 18
Mona Lisa Is Sold to the King of France   86

WEEK 19
Hattie Caraway Becomes First Woman Elected
to the U.S. Senate   91

WEEK 20
Charles Dow Develops a Stock-Picking Index
in Use More Than a Century Later   96

WEEK 21
Max Lauffer Invites Jonas Salk to Establish His
Lab at the University of Pittsburgh   101

WEEK 22
Emily Post Begins Work on *Etiquette*   106

WEEK 23
Allies Invade Normandy in World's Largest
Military Battle   110

WEEK 24
The Beatles Audition with George Martin   115

WEEK 25
Charles Darwin's "Pencil Sketches" Reveal
First Theories of Natural Selection   120

WEEK 26
Lakota, Cheyenne, and Arapaho Annihilate
Custer and His Men at Little Bighorn   125

WEEK 27
America's Founding Fathers Deflect Differences
to Achieve Common Goal   130

WEEK 28
The Berlin Wall Symbolizes a Culture of Fear   135

WEEK 29
John Roberts Becomes Black Bart   140

WEEK 30
Edward Whymper and His Team Are the First
Climbers to Ascend the Matterhorn   144

WEEK 31
Vince Lombardi Holds First Practice with the
Green Bay Packers   149

WEEK 32
Andrew Hamilton Presents Novel Defense in
John Peter Zenger Libel Trial   154

WEEK 33
Steve Jobs Rescues Apple from Insolvency   159

WEEK 34
Doane Robinson Persuades Gutzon Borglum
to Travel to the Black Hills   164

WEEK 35
Martin Luther King Jr. Delivers "I Have a
Dream" Speech   169

WEEK 36
Branch Rickey Signs Jackie Robinson to
Shatter Baseball's Color Barrier   174

WEEK 37
Frank Capra Buys the Rights to *It's a Wonderful Life*   179

WEEK 38
Two Years of Civil War Produce a New and
Improved Magna Carta   184

WEEK 39
Mary Edwards Walker Relishes Roles as a
Suffragist, Surgeon, and Spy   189

WEEK 40
Walt Disney Invites His Banker to Private
Screening of *Snow White and the Seven Dwarfs*   194

WEEK 41
Benjamin Franklin Convenes First Junto Club
in Philadelphia   199

WEEK 42
John F. Kennedy and Nikita Khrushchev End Cuban
Missile Crisis   204

WEEK 43
Henry V Defeats the Odds, Leading His Army
to Victory at Agincourt   209

WEEK 44
Sir Ernest Shackleton Gives Order to "Abandon Ship"   214

WEEK 45
George Washington Bids Farewell to His Troops   219

WEEK 46
Herbert Hoover Designates a Permanent Place
for Relaxing   224

WEEK 47
Viktor Frankl Tests His Theory on Himself in a
Concentration Camp   229

WEEK 48
Nelson Mandela Opens Anti-Apartheid Talks from Prison   234

WEEK 49
Sam Walton Hires His First Partner to Support Aggressive
Expansion Plan   239

WEEK 50
Marie Curie Defies the Royal Swedish Academy of Sciences   244

WEEK 51
Jesse Owens Wins Unprecedented Fourth Gold Medal at
Berlin Olympics   249

WEEK 52
Henry Ford Doubles Workers' Wages   254

ACKNOWLEDGMENTS   259
ABOUT THE AUTHOR   261
BIBLIOGRAPHY   263

"If you want to understand today, you have to search yesterday."
—PEARL S. BUCK

"There are no great men. There are only great challenges, which ordinary men like you and me are forced by circumstances to meet."
—ADMIRAL WILLIAM F. "BULL" HALSEY

"The most difficult thing is the decision to act, the rest is merely tenacity. The fears are paper tigers. You can do anything you decide to do."
—AMELIA EARHART

Preface

> "It is the characteristic excellence of the strong man that he can bring momentous issues to the fore and make a decision about them. The weak are always forced to decide between alternatives they have not chosen themselves."
>
> **—DIETRICH BONHOEFFER**

Every day, in enterprises large and small, leaders face issues that can make or break their organization and reputation because of a decision they will make—including the decision to do nothing.

Leadership is under the microscope, particularly in today's divisive, politically charged environment. Leadership has never been more important, and decision-making has rarely mattered more.

Fifteen years ago, I was invited to become a chair for Vistage International, the world's largest CEO membership organization with more than twenty-one thousand members in seventeen countries. Once a month, I facilitate three group meetings comprising of thirty-two CEOs and eighteen key executives in noncompeting businesses who are committed to improving professionally and personally. I conduct private coaching sessions with these executives. I speak to groups of executives all over the world an average of three times per month and hear directly from them as they wrestle with decision-making. Additionally, the strategic planning sessions I lead expose me to the hopes, fears, and frustrations of leadership teams in numerous industries.

From this unique vantage point as a coach, consultant, and confidant, I see firsthand that even the most successful leaders struggle with decision-making. And once the decision has been made, leaders encounter obstacles that test their commitment and discipline to execute their decision and achieve the outcome they envision. Making the decision is worth nothing without executing it.

Leadership: When Events and Decisions Collide

> "If past history was all there was to the game, the richest people would be librarians."
>
> **—WARREN BUFFETT**

While every person makes hundreds of decisions every day, leaders distinguish themselves in their decision-making: the stakes are almost always higher, the number of people affected by their decisions greater, and the responsibility to make the decision is theirs alone. To be a leader, you must make decisions.

Colonel John Boyd modeled decision-making in what's known as the OODA loop: "Observe-Orient-Decide-Act," where "time is the dominant parameter." The leader "who goes through the OODA loop in the shortest cycle prevails," noted F-16 designer Harry Hillaker, "because his opponent is caught responding to situations that have already changed."

Leaders don't always make the right decision. At the front end of most choices, it's impossible to know all of the things that will happen as a result of a single decision. Yet leaders are compelled to decide without fully knowing the consequences of their choices. Decision-making comes with the territory. Successful leaders learn from a bad decision and make a better decision the next time. Exceptional leaders make more good decisions than others when the stakes are the highest.

This book was inspired by responses I received from leaders around the world to blogs I've written on leadership lessons drawn from some of history's greatest triumphs and tragedies. A leader's character and decision-making ability is revealed during extreme conditions. How leaders respond during these moments is at the absolute heart of their story.

These insightful, stirring stories prompt today's leaders to reflect on their own situation as they seek to replicate the actions of men and women who made a courageous decision in the face of difficult circumstances and changed history. It's as if today's leaders are saying to themselves, *If ordinary people placed in extraordinary circumstances can summon the wisdom and courage to make a tough decision, perhaps I can channel their experience and energy to make a tough decision in the circumstances I'm facing.*

I also believe it's just as helpful to read cautionary tales reminding us of the dangers of hubris, false assumptions, and creating a culture where standing up for your beliefs can be a career-limiting move.

Good leaders are students of history and they love a good story. Even better if they can soak up a little history in a story relevant to their business that takes just ten minutes to read. This book provides you with inspiring examples of leadership and decision-making in bite-sized formats that prompt you to internalize your learning and record your thoughts at a pace of one lesson per week.

How the Entries Were Selected

> "History is a gallery of pictures in which there are few originals and many copies."
>
> **—ALEXIS DE TOCQUEVILLE**

Each of the fifty-two vignettes (one for each week of the year) illuminates decision-making by leaders in some of the biggest moments in history: in peacetime, in battle, in business, sports, science, technology, government, the arts, and in the otherwise ordinary routine of daily life. The principles, approaches, and insights examined in this book work for any leader in any organization. The lessons transcend size of organization or team, field of endeavor, geography, and time.

This book is not intended to be a scholarly work, though the facts supporting each of the fifty-two vignettes have been established by scholars, historians, journalists, and others. Their work is recognized and recommended in the bibliography.

I've combed through more than twenty-five thousand events to uncover little-known or oft-obscured circumstances where, in each case, a leader faced a decision that, once made, reverberated around their world—if not the entire world. I identified the key decision a leader made that ultimately led to triumph or tragedy. In many instances, it's likely you know about the event or person, but you may be less familiar with the context surrounding the decision. It's less likely you've paused to consider the implication of that decision from the perspective of what's happening today in your world.

This book is not a collection of anniversary dates. So the

April 15, 1912, sinking of *Titanic* is not this book's focus, but rather the decision made twenty-seven months earlier by Bruce Ismay, managing director of the White Star Line (the company that commissioned *Titanic*), to enlarge the ship's grand staircase. This decision meant each bulkhead of the sixteen watertight compartments was lowered so that when *Titanic* collided with the iceberg, the forward compartments were flooded within 160 minutes, sinking a ship that many considered unsinkable.

Of all the criteria for selecting events, the most challenging step became a matter of identifying a particular puzzle piece of history and placing that puzzle piece in chronological order as the event (regardless of year) occurred during a particular month. There are five stories for each of the five weeks in January, four for February, and so on. Notable events occur in every month, so the biggest decisions involving the biggest risks of power, prestige, money, and, in several instances, loss of life are included. For instance, James Burke's October 5, 1982, decision to recall thirty-one million bottles of Tylenol following seven deaths in the face of what many believed would kill the brand gave way to President Kennedy's October 1962 decisions during the Cuban missile crisis to avert nuclear war with Russia.

The Leader Must Decide

"You get whatever accomplishment you are willing to declare."

—GEORGIA O'KEEFFE

In all fifty-two entries, the events and leaders selected represent the zenith or nadir of decision-making and are showcased to invite today's leaders to reflect, connect the dots to their own situation, and then make informed decisions on matters they may have avoided or considered insoluble.

Each of us has flaws, and the men and women profiled here are no different. Thomas Jefferson wrote eloquently of liberty yet kept slaves; Franklin D. Roosevelt, John F. Kennedy, Martin Luther King Jr., and Nelson Mandela were unfaithful to their wives; Walt Disney and Henry Ford faced accusations of anti-Semitism; Marie Curie had an affair with her late husband's married student. "No man is a hero to his valet," quipped Anne-Marie Bigot de Cornuel, the one-time mistress of King Louis XIV.

But for all of these flaws, at a crucial moment in their lives— and in the lives of others who had placed their trust in them— these men and women found themselves alone as they considered the risks; weighed their options; confronted their beliefs, hopes, and fears; and ultimately made a profound decision that changed history's trajectory.

There's no single silver bullet for making difficult decisions. In my work with leaders (and in my own consulting practice), I recognize that leaders often make the tough decisions when the pain of not making them becomes greater than the pain of making them.

The point for all of us is that it is the decision to decide that matters.

Introduction

> "We sow our thoughts, and we reap our actions; we sow our actions, and we reap our habits; we sow our habits, and we reap our characters; we sow our characters, and we reap our destiny."
>
> **—DESIDERIUS ERASMUS**

Leadership is *hard*.

The ultimate responsibility for the success or failure of your team, department, or organization is in your hands. People are counting on you to put them in a position to succeed.

To lead effectively, to inspire people to do more than they think they can do, you're making decisions every day. Some decisions are bigger than others. And some are tougher than others. Few of the momentous decisions you'll make present choices as starkly drawn as "yes" or "no," "now" or "later," or "this" or "that."

How do you establish a framework for ethical decision-making? How do you communicate and instill this framework throughout your organization so it becomes second nature? How do you ensure the decisions you make will yield the results you expect? What do you do if you make a bad decision? How do you respond to controversy, crises, and setbacks?

The leaders you will meet in this book wrestled with these

types of questions. The circumstances they faced and the decisions they made in their moment of truth can guide you as you make yours.

How to Use This Book

> "In any moment of decision, the best thing you can do is the right thing, the next best thing is the wrong thing, and the worst thing you can do is nothing."
>
> **—THEODORE ROOSEVELT**

Most of the leaders I work with meet as noncompeting peers for a full day every month. In between these monthly group meetings, I meet with leaders in one-on-one executive coaching sessions or am invited to participate in senior management team meetings. This type of twice-a-month schedule works well in terms of establishing a rhythm for moving things along, keeping people informed, and providing an accountability support system to ensure the commitments executives make are honored.

But what happens in between these semi-monthly check-ins? Would a more frequent cadence be better?

Some leaders use daily diaries, journals, and time sheets to list their activities, record their allocation of time, and jot down their thoughts. Some leaders I work with use these types of journals and love them. As a consultant, I hated daily timekeeping. So I'm biased against a daily diary, which seems to me to be a bit of overkill.

I believe a weekly approach strikes the right balance for any leader who is committed to decision-making and the discipline of following through on their decision, and so that's how I've organized this book.

The entries you'll find in the following pages are intended to be read week by week—not several entries in one sitting, nor for extended periods of time. This book is filled with leadership insights, and these insights should be used to help you make better decisions in a range of circumstances. For about ten minutes per week, you can tap into a quick history lesson and then spend another five or ten minutes recording your thoughts to the questions posed in each entry.

You can start at the beginning of the book, or turn to the entry that corresponds to the week or month when you're reading the entry, or pick an entry that examines a subject that's of particular interest to you.

This book condenses some of history's greatest events into a single volume. If you are interested in learning more about a particular person or event, the bibliography (for the most part, full-length books) provides a terrific reading list.

Use this book for yourself. Answer the questions posed in each of the fifty-two entries as part of a process to help you focus your thinking and determine your course of action on a decision you're facing now or in the future.

You also can use this book as a guide with your colleagues to help your team examine decisions that need to be made for your department, division, or entire business enterprise. You may also choose to use the book with any other group that you believe would benefit from reviewing the entries and then answering thought-provoking questions.

This is a book you can return to again and again. The issues examined in the fifty-two vignettes are both perennial and universal. So you likely will find that revisiting the book—and, more important, your thoughts—can be helpful in further clarifying your thinking about certain scenarios, issues, and opportunities. Multiple readings will shed new light on matters requiring your decision, and will enable your thinking to evolve so that you are more confident in your conclusions. Bolstering your confidence is the fact that the implications of each decision examined is clearly evident. Time has rendered its verdict.

Decide whether it's helpful along your journey of self-discovery to share some of your conclusions with loved ones, trusted advisers, or your most intimate of friends. Any person that cares about you will be honored to play the role of sounding board, brainstorm resource, or accountability partner as you sort through the issues associated with historic events in this book.

My expectations for what you'll get out of this book are twofold: First, that this process will prompt you to reflect on important issues similar to yours that other leaders have confronted. Second, that, having made your decision, you'll take action to begin moving forward and achieve your goals.

After all, it's the leader's job to make decisions.

I am hopeful this book will be helpful to you when it's time for you to decide.

Bruce Ismay Reviews the Designs of *Titanic*

How a Series of Seemingly Insignificant Decisions Proved Catastrophic

> "I cannot conceive of any vital disaster happening to this vessel. Modern shipbuilding has gone beyond that."
> **—CAPTAIN EDWARD SMITH, COMMANDER, *TITANIC***

On a brisk Belfast day in January 1910, design considerations concerning the world's largest ship were being deliberated.

Decisions made that day by Bruce Ismay contributed to the deadliest peacetime maritime disaster in history twenty-seven months later when *Titanic* struck an iceberg and 1,514 people died.

Titanic was a floating hotel boasting the highest standards of luxury, including a swimming pool, squash courts, and ship-to-shore communication. "She was," said Ismay, "the latest thing in the art of shipbuilding."

As managing director of the White Star Line, Ismay was offering an extravagant seagoing experience in response to his competition's—Cunard Line—emphasis on speed. On July 29, 1908, Ismay approved drawings for the *Olympic*-class ocean liner and two days later signed letters of agreement authorizing construction, which began on March 31, 1909. Alexander Carlisle, construction company Harland & Wolff's chief designer, led the project. When finished, *Titanic* measured 882 feet (269 m) long with a maximum breadth of 92 feet 6 inches (28.19 m). Her height from keel to bridge was 104 feet (32 m) and she weighed 46,328 gross register tons.

Two seemingly insignificant decisions made in a matter of minutes that January day in 1910 would become catastrophic.

Ismay's decision to enlarge the grand staircase lowered bulkheads separating each of *Titanic*'s sixteen watertight compartments, creating a lower—and faster—flooding threshold in the ship's forward compartments where the collision occurred.

Though 1910 ships had quadrupled in size since 1908, safety regulations remained unchanged. Carlisle anticipated more lifeboats would be required on *Titanic* and presented plans that January day for forty-eight lifeboats. While the twenty lifeboats aboard *Titanic* exceeded requirements, maximum capacity was 1,176 people, half *Titanic*'s crew and passengers. Ismay approved Carlisle's plan to install davits for additional lifeboats, but decided against "cluttering" the deck with twenty-eight additional lifeboats unless regulations changed.

➡ **Every organization is susceptible to catastrophe, though risks may seem unlikely or insignificant. When did you last test your assumptions? Where are you vulnerable?**

At New York's Waldorf-Astoria Hotel four days after *Titanic* sunk, Ismay testified before an inquiry led by U.S. senator William Alden Smith that "absolutely no money was spared in her construction."

Money wasn't the primary concern. Shortages of time, talent, and materials were, and each figured into *Titanic's* demise.

With *Titanic's* construction behind schedule, hiring more riveters to meet the March 20, 1912, departure was an important agenda item at Harland & Wolff's October 28, 1911, board meeting. Steel rivets were stronger but were scarce and required machines for installation; *Titanic's* enormous curved bow prevented this machinery's use. Wrought iron rivets—three million of them—fastened *Titanic's* hull plates. Metallurgy specialists examining forty-six rivets retrieved from the wreck found three times more slag than modern wrought iron: *Titanic's* rivets were brittle, prone to breaking under pressure. The 1985 discovery of *Titanic's* wreck revealed her sinking was caused not by a large gash from the iceberg but rather six narrow slits where bow plates fitted with these weaker wrought iron rivets popped like champagne corks as the ship grazed the iceberg.

Ismay believed that had *Titanic* met the iceberg directly the ship "might not have sunk," but added, "it would have taken a very brave man to have kept his ship going straight on an iceberg."

With passenger safety taken for granted, *Titanic's* captain steamed at full speed despite six ice warnings. The American inquiry concluded that too much arrogance and not enough common sense proved fatal: "No general discussion took place among the officers; no conference was called to consider these warnings. The speed was not relaxed, the lookout was not increased, and the only vigilance displayed by the officer of the watch was by instructions to the lookouts to keep 'a sharp lookout for ice.'"

When Second Officer David Blair left *Titanic* before it sailed, he inadvertently took with him the key to the crow's nest locker where the binoculars were stored. Crewman Frederick Fleet, on duty as a lookout in the crow's nest at the time of the collision, testified he requested binoculars but was told "there is none."

"Suppose," Senator Smith asked Fleet, "you had had glasses… could you have seen this black object [the iceberg] at a greater distance?"

"We could have seen it a bit sooner," Fleet replied.

"How much sooner?"

"Well, enough to get out of the way."

Outdated standards, inadequate procedures, and lack of preparation sealed the passengers' fate.

Sixty minutes passed between the collision and launching the lifeboats. As each minute passed, four hundred tons of seawater poured into *Titanic*. She sank 160 minutes after the collision.

> ➡ **What procedures, systems, and safeguards are in place to detect changes—large and small—that can wreck your plan? When were these systems last tested? How will you address significant failures in your business plan and disasters in your workplace?**

Inquiries held in America and Great Britain concluded long-standing practices deemed safe were followed.

"What was a mistake in the case of the *Titanic*," the British inquiry warned, "would without doubt be negligence in any similar case in the future." New maritime regulations mandated more lifeboats, lifeboat drills, and round-the-clock wireless operation on passenger ships.

Eyewitnesses reported most passengers acted bravely, with men honoring the "women and children first" code.

Bruce Ismay, vilified for leaving the ship, was absolved by the British inquiry: "No other people were there at the time. There was room for him and he jumped in. Had he not jumped in he would merely have added one more life, namely, his own, to the number of those lost." Ismay's reputation never recovered. He was forty-nine.

Stanley Lord, commanding *Californian*, less than 19 miles (30.58 km) away from *Titanic*, ignored distress signals and took no action. His conduct was deemed "reprehensible."

Arthur Henry Rostron, commanding *Carpathia*, steaming 58 miles (93.34 km) through ice fields at night and rescuing 706 survivors, was "deserving of the highest praise."

⇒ **How would you and your leaders respond to adversity?**

As the captain of your ship, you must watch for and respect threats that could spell disaster.

Alfred Nobel Reimagines His Legacy

How Seeing His Future Caused the Merchant of Death to Create a Legacy of Peace

> "I intend to leave after my death a large fund for the promotion of the peace idea, but I am skeptical as to its results."
>
> **—ALFRED NOBEL**

Few of us have the opportunity to read our obituary while we're still alive.

What Alfred Nobel read in an April 1888 Paris newspaper struck him like a scene from Charles Dickens's *A Christmas Carol* when the Ghost of Christmas Yet to Come visits Scrooge and reveals people gloating over the penny-pinching miser's death.

In seeking to report the April 12 death of Alfred's fifty-six-year-old brother Ludvig, the newspaper erroneously exchanged Ludvig's life story with Alfred's, told that morning under the headline "The Merchant of Death Is Dead." Alfred Nobel was best known as the inventor of dynamite.

This harsh summary of Alfred's life introduced into the mind of one of the world's wealthiest men the repugnant possibility that, despite his pacifist leanings and intention that dynamite be used for commercial purposes, he would forever be remembered as a murderer.

Perhaps for the first time, and certainly not the last, Alfred Nobel, fifty-four, began thinking of possibilities for doing something "idealistic" that, nearly five years later, would lead him to bequeath the majority of his vast fortune to create and sustain the world's ultimate recognition of peace.

➡ Do the profits you make allow you to sleep soundly at night? What baggage must you unload that may be preventing you from being fully engaged, fully effective, and fully alive?

In December 1837, Alfred's father, Immanuel, departed for Finland to seek his fortune and avoid debtor's prison from his failed ventures, leaving his wife Caroline Andrietta and their three young boys in Sweden. Alfred was four years old.

Caroline opened a store selling dairy products and vegetables, securing her family's survival. The three boys attended a school for underprivileged children. Despite these hardships—or perhaps because of them—Alfred poured himself into his studies, excelling at comprehending difficult subjects, applying his learning to practical matters, and maintaining a tireless stamina despite frail health.

Immanuel, meanwhile, built a thriving business from his invention of explosive mines for land and sea defense, and in

December 1838 accepted Czar Nicholas I's invitation to move his business to St. Petersburg. In 1842, Immanuel sent for his family.

Upon their reunion, Immanuel hired tutors for his sons and summarized his boys' character: "Ludvig has the most brains, Alfred the greatest discipline, and Robert the greatest sense of enterprise." Alfred ultimately demonstrated he possessed the most potent combination of brains, discipline, and enterprise.

Chemistry fascinated Alfred. His high standards, fertile mind, and self-discipline propelled him past his older brothers in every academic endeavor. By age sixteen he'd become a brilliant chemist, and his impoverished childhood made Alfred a tough-minded entrepreneur focused on monetizing his family's inventions.

"If I come up with three hundred ideas in a year and only one of them is useful," he later mused, "I am content."

By the time of Alfred's death, he held 355 different patents and oversaw ninety different companies.

> ➡ **When did your organization last introduce a new product or service? What would you improve about your process to drive innovation?**

Russia's loss in the Crimean war ruined the Nobel business.

Having focused on producing armaments, the company was unable to pivot toward peacetime products and declared bankruptcy. The family returned to Sweden.

There, in a kitchen-turned-laboratory in a modest apartment shared with his brother Robert, Alfred invented a gas meter measuring liquids: his first patent. He was twenty-four years old. During the next two years, Alfred received two more patents and began experimenting with ways to control nitroglycerin's ferocious power.

On September 3, 1864, Alfred's younger brother Emil died when their nitroglycerin laboratory exploded. Alfred never spoke of this incident; the next day he was back at work. More nitroglycerin factories were built, and three years later Alfred was awarded Swedish patent number 102 for "dynamite or Nobel's safety powder." Alfred had tamed nitroglycerin's power.

Alfred's invention made him a wealthy industrialist. But he found himself alone.

Alfred, now forty-three, hired Bertha Kinsky as his secretary. She found Alfred "alternately sad and humorous"; Alfred found Bertha beautiful and intelligent. Within days, he proposed. She demurred. A week later, Alfred left Paris on business. When he returned, Bertha was gone.

Despite his heartbreak, Alfred remained friends with Bertha the rest of his life. In 1889, Bertha, now an Austrian baroness, published *Lay Down Your Arms!* denouncing the nascent arms race, which Alfred called "the wretched trade." Her book was published in twelve languages. Bertha became a leading figure in the peace movement.

Bertha invited Alfred to her 1892 Peace Conference in Bern. Though he made a small donation, he told her "good intentions alone will not assure peace." Nevertheless, Alfred attended. The conference added another particle of doubt to the premature obituary published four years earlier as Alfred contemplated his legacy.

On January 7, 1893, Alfred made his decision, writing to Bertha that he "would like to bequeath part of my fortune for the establishment of peace prizes."

When Alfred died on December 10, 1896, his will was opened eight days later, revealing 64 percent of his estate was bequeathed to the Royal Swedish Academy of Sciences. Prizes in Chemistry, Literature, Peace, Physics, and Medicine were first awarded in 1901.

➡ **If you were honored for your life's work, what achievement would you celebrate? What legacy would you leave?**

Alfred Nobel's efforts have not halted war. But every December 10, we salute those who have made "the most important pioneering discoveries or works in the field of knowledge and progress."

Julius Caesar Crosses the Rubicon

How Crossing a Small Stream in Italy Jump-Started the Roman Empire

| "The die is cast."

—JULIUS CAESAR

Achieving your goals despite difficult circumstances requires, above all, a resolute mindset.

Julius Caesar overcame substantial setbacks early in life to become one of the world's most accomplished generals before ascending to unprecedented levels of power in the Roman Republic, eventually governing the entire Mediterranean world in Europe, Africa, and Asia from the world's largest city—Rome. He ruled 20 percent of the world's population.

Caesar was well-educated, intelligent, quick-witted, a skilled warrior, an accomplished orator, and a consummate politician. He was, especially, a man of action.

Caesar was born into a patrician family that, despite

aristocratic longevity, was not influential politically. Like all aristocratic children, Caesar was raised to believe he was special and held to the highest Roman standards of dignity, piety, and virtue.

Before Caesar was sixteen, his father died; Caesar became the family patriarch. He quickly displayed the self-confidence that would mark his life, canceling a prearranged marriage and marrying Cornelia, daughter of Rome's most powerful man.

As a senator, Caesar prosecuted powerful men and, despite impressive arguments, lost cases where outcomes were predetermined.

Having made potent enemies, Caesar left Rome for Rhodes. Pirates captured his boat and ransomed him. Far from frightened, Caesar held the pirates "in disdain." With the ransom paid, Caesar organized a party of warships, pursued his former captors, and brought them to justice. Although he had no legal authority, Caesar ordered the pirates crucified. His version of mercy was having their throats cut rather than subjecting them to the painful death of crucifixion. He was twenty-four years old.

> ⇒ **What do you want to achieve in the next twelve months? What leadership habit will you improve?**

When Rome was overrun by Lucius Cornelius Sulla, a Roman general chafing from being bypassed for command, Sulla executed dozens of senators. Sulla demanded that Caesar divorce Cornelia. Caesar refused and fled, but upon his capture remained unbowed. At the behest of Caesar's mother, Sulla spared Caesar's life, noting the young man's ambition and warning Caesar "will one day destroy" Rome's rulers.

Wary of living in Rome while Sulla was alive, Caesar joined the army, serving with distinction in Asia and Cilicia.

Upon Sulla's death, Caesar returned to Rome and was elected military tribune, the starting point for a career mixing politics and soldiering. Following Cornelia's death in 69 BC, Caesar, thirty-one, served in Spain, ruefully observing a statue of Alexander the Great, who by age thirty-three had conquered the known world. Caesar's ambition grew.

In 63 BC, Caesar defeated two powerful senators for the post of Pontifex Maximus, chief priest of the Roman religion. Caesar's subsequent military campaign in Spain was victorious; his troops revered him.

Relentlessly ambitious and now wealthy from campaigning, Caesar sought and won election as consul, the Republic's highest elected office. Frustrated by senators blocking their legislation, Crassus (Rome's wealthiest man), Pompey (Rome's foremost general), and Caesar (whose military and political standing was second only to Pompey's) formed the First Triumvirate.

Upon Crassus's death in 53 BC, Pompey and Caesar's rivalry heightened; the alliance dissolved. "Caesar could not accept a superior," wrote Roman poet Lucan, "nor Pompey an equal."

By now, Caesar had spent eight years fighting the Gallic tribes in present-day France, Germany, and Switzerland. He was ready to return home and stand for election as consul. Pompey encouraged the Senate to order Caesar to disband his army. Caesar refused, fearing retribution. Pompey accused Caesar of treason. Each suspected the other of fomenting civil war.

On January 11, 49 BC, Caesar and his cohorts reached the river Rubicon where Caesar's province ended. "Even now," Roman historian Suetonius quotes Caesar as saying, "we could turn back; but once we cross that tiny bridge, then everything will depend on armed force."

"Crossing the Rubicon" has come to mean a decision from which there's no return. Caesar knew the risk. His men did, too. They stood with him.

> ➡ **Why do people listen to you? Why should they?**

Though Caesar's army was vastly outnumbered, Pompey and many senators fled.

Caesar defeated Pompey's lieutenants in Spain and Greece. Caesar pursued Pompey to Egypt, becoming Cleopatra's lover, joining forces with her army, and defeating Pharaoh at the Battle of the Nile. Pompey was assassinated by Pharaoh's followers.

When Caesar returned to Rome as dictator, he addressed the Senate:

> Many of you wished me dead. Many of you perhaps still do. But I hold no grudges and seek no revenge. I demand only this: …that you join with me in building a new Rome, a Rome that offers justice, peace, and land to all its citizens, not just the privileged few. Support me in this task, and old divisions will be forgotten. Oppose me, and Rome will not forgive you a second time. Senators, the war is over.

Then as now, there are people who say "yes" to your face and "no" with their actions.

Caesar was warned "Beware the Ides of March." Passing the

soothsayer on his way to the Theatre of Pompey where he would be stabbed to death, Caesar joked, "The Ides of March have come," believing the prophecy would not be fulfilled. "Aye, Caesar," replied the soothsayer, "but not gone."

> ⇒ Who do you believe or suspect is working against you? What's your evidence? What will you do?

From 49 to 44 BC, Caesar developed a new constitution, ordered a census, established a police force, and, most impressively, installed the Julian calendar.

Caesar's crossing of the Rubicon marked the end of the Roman Republic and paved the way for the Roman Empire.

A Letter Triggers William McKnight's Curiosity and Launches an Empire

How Curiosity Sparked 3M's Culture of Innovation

> "If you put fences around people, you get sheep. Give people the room they need."
>
> **—WILLIAM McKNIGHT**

3M is one of the world's most innovative companies, having generated more than one hundred thousand patents since its 1902 founding.

But in 1904, the five founders' investment of time, money, and hard work in the Minnesota Mining and Manufacturing Company wasn't enough. The company was failing. Their first sale of corundum in March was their last. Three years would pass before the mistake was discovered: company mines did not contain corundum but anorthosite, a commercially worthless mineral.

Despite personal success outside 3M, the founders' efforts could not reverse the company's fortunes. By November 1904, the company had no funds to continue operations and faced mounting debt. To save 3M, the founders agreed to sell controlling interest to raise cash. But who would invest in this struggling enterprise?

In January 1905, 3M shareholder Edgar Ober paused over breakfast as he read a letter from his friend and 3M founder John Dwan outlining the company's dire situation. Ober believed the company should abandon mining and start manufacturing abrasives. It would take $14,000 to settle debts and another $25,000 to start a factory. Ober was prepared to invest beyond his initial $5,000 outlay but needed a partner. He met that morning with businessman Lucius Ordway, persuading him to invest. Ordway had one caveat: he wanted "nothing to do with running the company."

Ober's March letter to Dwan outlined terms for purchasing controlling interest. At the May 1905 annual meeting, Ober was named 3M's new president. Apart from one three-year break, Ober served as president until 1929—the first eleven years without compensation.

In January 1906, sandpaper orders dribbled in but expenses outpaced sales. By November, Ordway had invested $200,000. There was no quit in 3M. But there was no profit in sight.

➡ **What causes you to continue supporting something that hasn't delivered the results you expect?**

To outsiders, 3M was the "largest sandpaper company in the world," but the enterprise was struggling.

When William McKnight applied for a job as assistant bookkeeper, he was so nervous his handwriting was illegible. McKnight was turned down. But on May 13, 1907, McKnight interviewed again and was hired for $11.55 a week. He would succeed Ober as 3M's president.

McKnight was observant, hardworking, and loyal. He was named the company's first cost accountant in 1909. He put two and two together, realizing 3M needed help selling products, cutting costs, and improving product quality. He attacked these problems with intelligence and energy. In 1911, he was named office manager of 3M's nascent Chicago office.

McKnight brought an obsession with quality and a disdain for discounting—philosophies that ultimately ensured both his and the company's future. He believed 3M should avoid highly competitive markets. In 1914, McKnight became 3M's general manager, distinguishing himself by developing product improvement processes and sticking to his principles during a five-year price war when competitors were "standing by, waiting for 3M to fail." In 1915, McKnight was elected vice president. He was twenty-nine years old.

Ober became McKnight's friend, mentor, and adviser. Through savvy decision-making by both men, 3M was debt-free by 1916. McKnight was 3M's missing ingredient. From the time he became general manager in 1914 until his 1966 retirement, 3M's sales increased by 17.1 percent on a compound annual growth rate basis—from $264,000 to $1.2 billion.

> → **How do you encourage those delivering the greatest impact? What else might you do to ensure your stars know their future is bright?**

William McKnight opened a letter one frosty day in January 1920 that would change the course of 3M's history.

Francis Okie's letter requested "samples of every mineral grit size you use in manufacturing sandpaper."

McKnight could've replied that 3M wasn't in the business of selling bulk minerals. He could've ignored Okie's letter. Instead, McKnight's curiosity was triggered.

Okie had invented waterproof sandpaper. But his investors lost interest when he couldn't obtain materials. Okie wrote to 3M wanting to buy "enough to get started." Learning of Okie's invention, McKnight initiated an eleven-month courtship culminating with Okie selling 3M the rights—and making 3M the global leader of abrasives.

McKnight valued the power of curiosity and believed sales were created not by leaving brochures with receptionists, but by talking with shop floor workers to learn what problems they encountered with competitive products. McKnight also drove collaboration between 3M's salesmen and its factory.

By 1925, 3M's policy manual warned "No plant can rest on its laurels—it either develops and improves or loses ground." In 1948, McKnight created the 15 percent rule: "3M technical employees are encouraged to devote up to 15 percent of their working hours to independent projects."

Before McKnight codified curiosity as a foundational value, inquisitiveness sparked the 1925 invention of masking tape and, in 1929, Scotch tape. McKnight also stipulated 30 percent of 3M's revenues must come from products invented within the past five years.

> ➡ What innovation has delivered the biggest impact to your customers or your organization? How can you get the best ideas from the most people?

3M generates billions of dollars by giving employees the freedom to spend nearly one full day each week daydreaming. "The mistakes that people will make," said McKnight, "are of much less importance than the mistake that management makes if it tells them exactly what to do."

Liddy, Mitchell, Dean, and Magruder Plan the Watergate Break-In

How a Toxic Culture Toppled the World's Most Powerful Man

> "Obviously, crime pays, or there'd be no crime."
>
> **—G. GORDON LIDDY**

Power brings out the best in some people. And the worst in others.

For Richard Nixon, the power of the presidency brought out his best...and his worst.

Nixon's accomplishments as president were impressive and unprecedented.

His 1972 Beijing trip established American diplomatic relations with China and that trip's success prompted talks the same year with the Soviet Union, resulting in a Cold War thaw and the signing of the Anti-Ballistic Missile Treaty. Nixon ended the unpopular Vietnam War.

At home, Nixon enacted wage and price controls to combat inflation, established the Environmental Protection Agency, and launched the War on Cancer.

But Nixon is the only American president to resign from office, and the Watergate scandal is the darkest chapter of his presidency and the one for which he's most remembered.

Four weeks after Nixon's 1969 inauguration, the North Vietnamese launched a new offensive against American forces in South Vietnam from their Cambodian "sanctuaries." Having campaigned to end the war, Nixon viewed this attack as a personal insult and vowed retaliation. "Without the Vietnam War," Nixon's Chief of Staff H. R. Haldeman observed, "there would have been no Watergate."

As Nixon considered his options, the Viet Cong attacked South Vietnam's capital on March 15. Nixon decided to bomb Cambodia. Concerned this move would fan America's anti-war flames, Nixon never consulted Congress, unleashing secret American bombing missions.

When the story of the secret bombings inevitably appeared on the *New York Times'* front page, Nixon went ballistic about the leaks. Determined to crack down on what he believed was a conspiracy to undermine his presidency, Nixon ordered the phones of thirteen White House, State, and Defense Department officials to be tapped by the FBI. "It is clear," Nixon told William Sullivan of the FBI, "that I don't have anybody in my office I can trust."

➡ **How does the way you think affect your organization's culture?**

Presidents John F. Kennedy and Lyndon B. Johnson ordered electronic eavesdropping.

What made Nixon's approach different was that when he couldn't convince the FBI and CIA to tap phones, he ordered those in his administration to do the dirty work.

Despite winning the 1968 election by just 1 percent, Nixon undertook a one-man crusade to reestablish America's preeminence. Welfare entitlements, the permissiveness of the sixties, and the Vietnam War cast a pall Nixon was determined to shake off. The generation gap sowed seeds of distrust in America, and Nixon's White House culture mirrored this distrust—or deepened it—with suspicion, schemes, and secrecy.

Nixon's presidency hit its "lowest point" in early 1971 with unemployment at its highest since 1961 and the dollar at its lowest since 1949. Vietnam was a quagmire.

Already thinking about his reelection and desperate to jump-start America's turnaround, Nixon proceeded to gather dirt on "enemies of the state," wielding this information as a weapon against political opponents—a failed strategy that would characterize behavior associated with the Watergate scandal.

Nixon's loss to Kennedy in 1960 by 113,000 votes amid rumors of voter fraud in Illinois and Texas—states Kennedy won—fueled Nixon's paranoia. "I vowed," Nixon wrote, "that I would never again enter an election at a disadvantage by being vulnerable."

On January 5, 1972, Nixon announced his candidacy for reelection.

Though Nixon would later deny direct knowledge of the Watergate break-in, those who worked for him read between the lines.

On January 27, 1972, Attorney General John Mitchell convened a meeting where G. Gordon Liddy presented plans to Mitchell, John Dean, and Jeb Magruder on undermining anti-war demonstrations, intercepting telephone traffic, and "ratfucking"— discrediting opponents by disseminating false or partly false accusations. Liddy also covered bugging the campaign headquarters of Democratic presidential nominees Edmund Muskie and George McGovern and the Democratic National Headquarters, located in Washington, DC's prestigious Watergate complex.

"Gordon," said John Mitchell, the nation's top law enforcement officer at this January meeting, "a million dollars is a hell of a lot of money. I'd like you to come back with something more realistic."

> ⇒ **List your personal values. How regularly do you use your values as a filter for decision-making? In what areas of your life can you be better at walking your talk?**

Failure is an orphan.

Watergate's failure spawned many versions of who knew what when. These facts are undisputed:

- Five men paid with reelection funds were arrested on June 17, 1972, for breaking into the Democratic National Committee headquarters at the Watergate complex.
- Names in the address books of those arrested led to the White House; a cover-up quickly followed. On August 29, Nixon said, "I can say categorically that...no one in the White House staff, no one in this Administration, presently employed, was involved."

- Bob Woodward and Carl Bernstein's October 10 *Washington Post* account reported FBI evidence indicating widespread political spying and sabotage.
- Nixon defeated George McGovern on November 11 in a landslide.
- G. Gordon Liddy and James McCord were convicted January 30, 1973.
- H. R. Haldeman, John Ehrlichman, and Attorney General Richard Kleindienst resigned April 30. John Dean was fired.
- The Senate Watergate committee began nationally televised hearings into the incidents on May 18.
- The Supreme Court ruled unanimously on July 24 for Nixon to release tape recordings of White House conversations. Three days later, the House Judiciary Committee passed the first of three articles of impeachment.
- Nixon resigned on August 8, succeeded by Vice President Gerald Ford.

"Everybody," said evangelist Billy Graham, "has a little bit of Watergate in him."

> ⇒ **What did you miss in the hiring process for the worst hire you ever made?**

Nixon was never charged and never served time. The Watergate scandal resulted in sixty-nine government officials being charged. Forty-eight were found guilty.

Watergate has become the scandal by which others are named.

Queen Elizabeth Declines to Marry, Producing No Heir to the Throne

How Lack of Succession Planning Placed the British Empire at Risk

> "Though the sex to which I belong is considered weak, you will nevertheless find me a rock that bends to no wind."
>
> **—ELIZABETH I**

Elizabeth, daughter of Henry VIII and Anne Boleyn, was dealt a bad hand.

Elizabeth's temperamental, womanizing father wanted to end his marriage with Anne to marry Jane Seymour. Henry's solution was to sever the Church of England's ties with Rome. With the stroke of a pen, Anne was no longer Henry's wife and Elizabeth was no longer his heir. Anne was tried on spurious charges of treason, predictably found guilty, and beheaded three days later.

Elizabeth was a princess one day and a bastard the next.

Her illegitimate position, suspected Protestant faith, and status as a woman made success improbable.

Yet Elizabeth's hunger to learn, formidable intellect, common-sense judgment, and willful mindset presented her with advantages amid her difficulties. She became fluent in Greek, French, Latin, Italian, Spanish, and Welsh. She was adept at needlepoint, played the lute, composed poetry, and was as talented on the dance floor as she was on the back of a horse or hunting in the woods.

Henry's death lifted his son Edward VI to the throne, beginning six years of economic hardship and rebellion. When Edward died at fifteen, he was succeeded by Mary, Elizabeth's half sister through Henry's first marriage. Mary's five-year reign was equally tumultuous as she ruthlessly reinstated Catholicism in England, executing more than three hundred Protestants and earning the sobriquet "Bloody Mary." Mary accused Elizabeth of being a Protestant and a conspirator in a failed coup. Though Elizabeth was innocent, she was locked in the Tower of London for three months, a traumatic experience where Elizabeth feared execution as each day dawned.

When Mary died childless on November 17, 1558, Elizabeth was proclaimed Queen of England. Elizabeth had prepared herself for this unlikely moment. She was twenty-five years old.

➡ **Where are you in a perilous position? What strengths will you rely on to claim the advantage?**

Elizabeth ascended to power against a backdrop of religious turmoil, staggering government debt, and threats of invasion from France and Spain.

England was isolated and vulnerable.

Elizabeth was determined to deliver peace and a stable government.

She had survived two brushes with death, experienced the executions of her mother and two of Henry's other wives, and seen others close to her sent to the gallows and the block. Elizabeth brought a clearheaded sense of reality to the throne. Caution was her watchword, moderation her approach, and subtlety her ally. "Video et taceo," Elizabeth would say in Latin: *I see but say nothing.*

Though she kept her own counsel (and kept everyone guessing), Elizabeth relied on a small group of trusted advisers: William Cecil, Thomas Radclyffe, Robert Dudley, and Francis Walsingham. Elizabeth played her cards expertly. She was the queen, and these four men her aces.

Elizabeth's first major test as queen occurred on February 6, 1559, three weeks after her coronation. A formal petition was presented encouraging her "to take a consort who might relieve her of those labors which are only fit for men." Male leaders wanted her to marry so her new husband could rule.

Affronted by this request, Elizabeth calmly replied, "I am already bound unto a husband, which is the kingdom of England."

Perhaps her views of marriage were influenced by her father's mistreatment of women. Perhaps remaining single offered political advantages, using marriage as a prize while avoiding the dangers a foreign-born husband would interject into her empire. Perhaps Elizabeth did not want to marry one of her subjects and risk creating factions. Perhaps her intellect and temper, like her mother's, made Elizabeth ill-suited for matrimony.

She would stick to her priorities. Marriage was not one of them.

"I would rather be a beggar and single," she said, "than a queen and married."

⇒ **What are your priorities? How can you be certain your colleagues are clear about your priorities?**

Elizabeth's unwillingness to marry continuously captured the imaginations of other nations' leaders and thoroughly frustrated her counselors.

Many believed her lack of succession planning placed the Empire at risk. Elizabeth was prepared to accept the distractions the succession question prompted in return for the advantages it brought England with princes and kings competing for her hand in marriage.

She knew what she was doing. Accused by some as indecisive, Elizabeth followed a deliberate strategy of playing for time to ensure peace and stability. Obfuscation, procrastination, and prevarication were her tools.

The decision she could not deflect involved her cousin, Mary Queen of Scots.

When Mary fled to England following an uprising in 1568, she expected Elizabeth to protect her. Yet Mary had coveted Elizabeth's crown as hers and repeatedly instigated plots to assassinate Elizabeth.

Elizabeth took Mary into protective custody, moving Mary to various castles over an eighteen-and-a-half-year period. When another assassination attempt on Elizabeth pointed to Mary, Parliament was unanimous in condemning Mary to death. It was an anguishing decision for Elizabeth. Signing Parliament's warrant would set a precedent for executing a monarch. Failing to act meant Mary posed a continued threat to national security.

On February 3, 1587, Elizabeth signed the warrant. The next day Mary was beheaded.

➡ **What difficult decision are you avoiding? What are you waiting for?**

When Elizabeth died at age sixty-nine, she had ruled for forty-five years and delivered peace and stability. During the Elizabethan era, England had taken its place at the head of European powers.

Reich Minister Speer Counters Hitler's Plan to Destroy Germany's Art and Infrastructure

How Guts and Guile Conquered Evil

> "One seldom recognizes the devil when he is putting his hand on your shoulder."
>
> **—ALBERT SPEER**

Every leader eventually answers for their actions.

In post-war Germany, Albert Speer faced Nuremberg prosecutors as one of the Third Reich's most powerful leaders.

Speer was an unlikely accomplice to evil. He was the product of an upper-middle-class family and followed in the footsteps of his father and grandfather, both respected architects. Speer joined the Nazi party in January 1931, believing he was not choosing a political ideology but, rather, "becoming a follower of Hitler, whose magnetic force had reached out to me."

Eighteen months later, Speer was selected to design the headquarters of the National Socialist Motor Corps, and by March 1933, following Adolf Hitler's election as chancellor, Speer was working full-time designing new government buildings. Speer was gratified his work pleased his clients, but, observing the unrefined traits of party members, thought, "A country cannot be governed by such people."

With Hitler's first party rally approaching, Speer was summoned to Nuremberg to make architectural recommendations. Local officials dared not to decide, sending Speer with his sketches to party headquarters in Munich. "Only the Fuehrer himself can decide this sort of thing," Speer was told in Munich before being dispatched to his first private meeting with Germany's chancellor. Hitler said nothing to Speer until, after reviewing the sketches, he approved them brusquely: "Agreed."

By autumn, Speer was overseeing renovations to Hitler's chancellery residence. Hitler visited the site daily and was guided by Speer, who soon realized what most people missed: Hitler was held "spellbound" by drawings and viewed architecture as a symbol of power.

"I became increasingly astonished to realize that before 1944," Speer recalled, "I so rarely—in fact almost never—found time to reflect about myself." Rereading Hitler's speeches that earlier had captivated him, Speer saw in hindsight that "Hitler openly aired his intention to pervert the meaning of the concept of culture by mobilizing it for his own power goals."

⇒ **What signals might you be choosing to ignore?**

When Speer's boss, Paul Troost, died in January 1934, Speer became the Nazi party's chief architect.

He was twenty-eight years old.

Hitler took particular interest in Speer, confiding, "I was looking for an architect to whom I could entrust my building plans. I wanted someone young; for as you know, these plans extend far into the future." Speer saw before him "the most exciting prospects a young architect can dream of" fortified by his relationship with Hitler.

For the 1934 rally, Speer was tasked with transforming the unattractive Zeppelin Field, the Nuremberg parade grounds seen in Leni Riefenstahl's propaganda film *Triumph of the Will*. Speer decided to hold the rally at night, lighting thousands of flags with searchlights aimed skyward. "The effect," wrote British ambassador Sir Nevile Henderson, "was both solemn and beautiful...like a cathedral of ice."

Hitler's popularity increased as Germans saw him as the architect of economic and foreign policy progress. Hitler, seeking "the biggest of everything to glorify his works and magnify his pride," saw Speer as the man to design and build monuments. Speer received the Grand Prix at the 1937 Paris World's Fair for his chancellery plans and shortly thereafter was appointed general building inspector for the Reich, answering only to Hitler.

Speer's relationship with Hitler sparked jealousy within Hitler's inner circle and imposed relentless pressure on Speer. Now married with children, Speer was compelled to move his family to

Hitler's Obersalzberg retreat, calling this situation "ruinous" to his work because of the isolation, boredom, and rigorous demands on Speer's time.

The morning after *Kristallnacht* in 1938, Speer drove past the smoldering ruins of Jewish synagogues. At the time, Speer recalled later, "I did not see that more was being smashed than glass."

Just as Faust bargained with the devil to exchange his soul for unlimited worldly pleasures, so, too, had Speer made his pact with Hitler.

⇒ **What are you trying to prove? How might you be bartering your life to prove it?**

Germany's wartime production was unsustainable.

When Minister of Armaments Fritz Todt died in February 1942, Hitler turned to Speer, whose remarkable peacetime results on impossibly short deadlines made him ideal to take over. Speer was charged with making bricks without straw.

For a while he succeeded. But Germany was losing the war.

Speer's epiphany occurred in early February 1945 when he realized Hitler was ordering Germany "to go heroically to its destruction"—the opposite of principles articulated in *Mein Kampf*. Speer "came to the decision to eliminate Hitler." Speer's plans to introduce poisonous gas into Hitler's Berlin bunker failed, so Speer undermined Hitler by issuing contradictory orders.

Hitler's "Nero Decree" of March 19, 1945, ordering all German art, infrastructure, and historic buildings destroyed was countermanded by Speer, who knew total annihilation would make Germany's post-war recovery more arduous.

Had Hitler known, Speer would have faced a firing squad. Instead, exactly six weeks later, Hitler was dead.

> ⇒ What's your response when a person who holds your future in their hands does something morally, ethically, or legally wrong?

By risking his life and defying Hitler at the war's end, Speer accelerated Germany's postwar recovery. He was spared the hangman's noose and sentenced to twenty years in prison.

Pope Gregory XIII Issues Papal Bull Reforming the Julian Calendar

How Smart Thinking and Bold Decision-Making Overcame Twelve Centuries of Inaccuracy and Inertia

> "We shall never have any more time. We have, and we have always had, all the time there is."
>
> **—ARNOLD BENNETT**

Time was slipping away.

Once Julius Caesar decreed the Roman Empire would mark the passage of time by a solar calendar in 45 BC, man-made dates on the new calendar began drifting away from nature's equinoxes and solstices—particularly the northern vernal equinox on which Easter's date is based.

Caesar's calendar—the Julian calendar—corrected the problem of manually adding days to the Roman calendar, which totaled 355 days. With the month of July already named for him, Caesar renamed the following month August, commemorating his greatest triumphs, and added a day each to July and August, making them the year's longest months. The two days were taken from February, leaving it with twenty-eight days.

The Julian calendar was more accurate, but it, too, was inexact, remaining slightly misaligned with nature, and, as a result, gaining about three days every four centuries.

Astronomers, mathematicians, popes, and emperors recognized this problem for centuries. How to correct it was the issue.

Festivals were linked with the passing seasons, so the Catholic Church stepped in to address the Julian calendar's inaccuracy with the aim of replacing pagan celebrations with holy days, or *holidays*.

In 325 AD, Roman emperor Constantine invited bishops throughout Christendom to Nicea (now İznik in Turkey) for an ecumenical Council patterned after the Roman Senate. One of the most significant outcomes of this Council was establishing the uniform observance of Easter's date, a decision that magnified the calendar's inaccuracy.

Time and energy were invested to decipher this problem; no proposal proved satisfactory.

➡ If you tracked your time in thirty-minute increments for a month, what would you find? How are you investing your time? Will this matter one year from now?

Resolving the Julian calendar's inaccuracy required the convergence of science, religion, and pragmatism.

What incorrect assumptions and mathematical errors were being made about the earth and moon's movements? How must any calculation align with the Council of Nicea decree that Easter and its related holy days would follow the spring equinox?

For twelve hundred years, astronomers, scientists, and mathematicians could not agree. Progress was realized during the sixteenth century when the Church invited Nicolaus Copernicus to state his views on the heavens. By 1532, Copernicus had largely completed *On the Revolutions of the Celestial Spheres* and his conclusions were received enthusiastically by Pope Clement VII. Copernicus's work was published in 1543, enabling Erasmus Reinhold to compute the Prutenic Tables in 1554, representing another step forward for calendar reform.

Among the scholars and clergy convening in 1563 for the Council of Trent was Cardinal Ugo Boncompagni. Upon the death of Pope Pius V in 1572, Cardinal Boncompagni was chosen pope, assuming the name of Gregory XIII in homage to the great reforming pope Gregory I. A former law professor, the new pope's approach to problems and his decisiveness were essential in reforming the calendar. He was seventy.

After twelve hundred years of debate, delay, and indecision, the ten-year process Gregory XIII initiated to fix the calendar was bold, focused, and comparatively speedy: First, the problem would be resolved once and for all. Second, small adjustments were unacceptable; a complete overhaul was required. Third, gradual implementation was not an option; once a decision was made, the reformed calendar would become the law of the land.

A proposal authored by Aloysius Lilius was presented to Gregory, who approved the concept of adding leap days as well as dropping ten days to sync the calendar and sun. The change would occur in October, owing to the month with the fewest religious observances. In 1577, *Compendium of the New Plan for Restoring the Calendar* was circulated for review among eminent scholars at the world's leading universities. Christopher Clavius made the final modifications.

In September 1580, the commission's recommendations were presented to Pope Gregory XIII, and on February 24, 1582, he signed the papal bull *Inter Gravissimas*. The reformed Julian calendar became the Gregorian calendar.

> ➡ **What persistent problem demands your decisive action?**

Measures of time have existed since the Paleolithic Age six thousand years ago.

Ancient Egyptians used obelisks. The first clocks appeared at the beginning of the fourteenth century. Personal watches followed one hundred years later.

Time is your most precious commodity. How do successful people manage it?

In 1910, Arnold Bennett wrote *How to Live on 24 Hours a Day*, offering these thoughts:

- ◆ Approach the twenty-four-hour day as two components: eight hours for work; the remaining sixteen hours as yours to be planned and utilized. "If your ordinary day's work is thus exhausting, then the balance of your life is wrong and must be adjusted."

◆ Claim ninety minutes an evening for three evenings. Start small, succeed, continue. "A glorious failure leads to nothing; a petty success may lead to a success that is not petty."

◆ Take time to reflect. "We do not reflect upon genuinely important things; upon the problem of our happiness, upon the main direction in which we are going."

⟹ **What must you do to reserve eight hours of time per week—every week—strictly for yourself? What must you do to make it possible to take a two-week vacation and unplug completely from the office?**

"The chief beauty about time," wrote Bennett, "is that you cannot waste it in advance. You can turn over a new leaf every hour if you choose."

Henri Dunant Forms the International Red Cross

How an Act of Conscience Elevated Compassion

> "[I have seen] the soul of a man leave this world in the grip of unimaginable agony."
>
> **—HENRI DUNANT**

Tragic events can inspire noble responses.

The formation of the International Red Cross traces its origins to one of history's bloodiest battles—the Battle of Solferino— where in a single day in Italy forty thousand Austrian, French, and Sardinian soldiers died or were left for dead. Another forty thousand soldiers died days later from infection, thirst, hunger, and shock.

Italy—divided for decades among France, Austria, Spain, and numerous independent Italian states—sought unification.

Napoleon III believed backing the Sardinians would bolster France's influence.

At dawn on June 24, 1859, Austrian and French regiments clashed, igniting fifteen continuous hours of combat among three hundred thousand troops and marking the last major European conflict led on the battlefield by monarchs.

Though evenly matched, neither army expected to fight that day. Soldiers from both camps had been force-marched to the battlefield on empty stomachs. Water rations ran dry. Summer's sun beat down mercilessly. Yet the soldiers fought on.

Henri Dunant, a Swiss businessman with companies operating in foreign colonies, had traveled to Solferino seeking Napoleon III's intervention on a water-rights contract in French-controlled Algeria where Dunant's company struggled to survive.

Arriving the day after the battle, Dunant witnessed "the most dreadful sights imaginable. Bodies of men and horses covered the battlefield; corpses were strewn over roads, ditches, ravines, thickets, and fields; the approaches of Solferino were literally thick with dead."

Little attention was accorded the dead, dying, and wounded.

Dunant organized civilians to care for injured soldiers, purchasing supplies with his own funds. He erected makeshift hospitals. Using the rallying cry "Tutti fratelli" (*All are brothers*), Dunant persuaded locals to tend the wounded irrespective of nationality, and he arranged for Austrian doctors captured by the French to be released. He was thirty-one.

➡ **What is your response to injustice? If you don't respond, who will?**

Henri Dunant grew up in one of Geneva's established families, imbued with piety, civic-mindedness, and compassion.

Upon entering Geneva's most prestigious school, Dunant's classwork did not foreshadow his calling. He was asked to leave because of poor grades.

Dunant apprenticed with the banking house Lullin et Sautter and was invited to remain with the firm. But his interest was torn between commerce and social causes.

In 1852, Dunant founded Geneva's YMCA, and when Harriet Beecher Stowe traveled to Geneva following the publication of *Uncle Tom's Cabin*, Dunant's meeting with the forty-one-year-old Stowe left a lasting impression.

The devastation Dunant witnessed at Solferino left a far deeper one. Faced with a failing business on the one hand and social injustice on the other, Dunant's decision was clear. Upon returning to Geneva, Dunant abandoned his business interests and began writing a book about his Solferino experiences.

Dunant's book—published with his own funds in 1862 as *A Memory of Solferino*—heralded his new calling with its solemn caution: "What has become of the love of glory which electrified this brave soldier at the commencement of the campaign…? Where is the irresistible allurement? Where the contagious enthusiasm, increased by the odor of powder…by the noise of cannon and the whistling of bullets which hide the view of danger, suffering, and death. In these many hospitals of Lombardy may be seen at what price is bought that which men so proudly call 'Glory,' and how dearly this glory costs."

The book earned immediate acclaim. Copies soon circulated in Paris, Turin, St. Petersburg, and Leipzig, read by princes, politicians, generals, and monarchs.

Dunant traveled ceaselessly, challenging convention with this question: "Would it not be possible to establish in every country of Europe, Aid Societies, whose aim would be to provide, during war, volunteer nurses for the wounded, without distinction of nationality?"

⇒ **If you had it to do over again—let's say you were just starting out—what would you do differently?**

Dunant labeled the Battle of Solferino "a European catastrophe."

General Guillaume Henri Dufour, a respected military strategist and politician, read Dunant's book and wrote to the young author, "It is most important that people read accounts like yours so that they can see what the glory of the battlefield costs in terms of pain and tears."

Geneva lawyer and philanthropist Gustave Moynier read the book and arranged to meet Dunant. The young lawyer invited Dunant to attend the next meeting of Geneva's Public Welfare Society, which also would be attended by General Dufour, the Society's former president.

On February 9, 1863, sandwiched between a discussion of new French classics and the founding of an agricultural colony for delinquent children was a proposal to fund a "corps of volunteer nurses for armies at war."

Discussion was not particularly enthusiastic, yet the following week, on February 17, 1863, five men from Geneva's most prominent families—General Dufour, Moynier, Dunant, and doctors Louis Appia and Théodore Maunoir—formed the International Committee for Relief to the Wounded.

The International Red Cross was born.

> ➡ **What kind of organization is yours trying to be? If your organization did not exist, what would the world be missing?**

Today, nearly one hundred million Red Cross volunteers, members, and staff worldwide provide humanitarian protection and assistance.

Dunant was the first recipient of the 1901 Nobel Peace Prize.

Colonel William B. Travis Gives His Alamo Defenders a Choice: Leave, or Stay and Die

How a Simple Question Changed Texas History

> "True courage is completing the things you say while cowardice is just saying the things you wish to complete."
>
> **—WILLIAM B. TRAVIS**

On March 2, 1836, Texas declared independence from Mexico.

Four days later, the Alamo fell.

While the vote for independence was significant, the Battle of the Alamo was the pivotal event in the Texas Revolution that—in spite of its failure, or perhaps because of it—captured the public's imagination and inspired the young Texas army as it defeated a larger, battle-tested Mexican army six weeks later.

For most leaders, few, if any, of your decisions will come down to life or death stakes. But you occasionally will need to rally your troops when the odds are stacked against you.

The Mexican government and American settlers in the Mexican province of Texas tolerated an uneasy relationship that deteriorated steadily from 1825 to 1835.

Texians were divided on their objective: gain independence from Mexico, or return to a way of life outlined in the Mexican Constitution of 1824? They all agreed the Mexican government was growing increasingly oppressive. When one hundred Mexican soldiers were dispatched to Gonzales in September 1835 to reclaim a cannon given to the settlers by the Mexican government to repel Comanche attacks, the Texians refused to return the cannon.

Their flag made clear their stance: "Come and Take It!"

The October 2, 1835, skirmish that ensued mattered little militarily. But it marked a clear break between the settlers and the Mexican government, ushering in the Texas Revolution. Exactly five months later, Texas declared its independence.

➡ How clear to everyone are your objectives?

As the New Year dawned on 1836, all Mexican troops had been driven out of the province.

President General Antonio López de Santa Anna was furious. He was determined to reclaim Texas and stop the rebellion. The focal point of Santa Anna's campaign was the Alamo mission situated near San Antonio de Bexar where one hundred Texians were garrisoned. On February 23, 1836, Santa Anna marched 1,500 soldiers into San Antonio. He divided another one thousand men to guard the routes out of San Antonio to Gonzales and Goliad as his first steps to retake Texas.

The commander of the Alamo was Colonel William B. Travis. Just twenty-six, he had distinguished himself as a leader who inspired his men and won battles. Aware of the growing peril, Travis wrote multiple letters from the Alamo appealing for reinforcements and supplies. The most famous of these, written February 24, was labeled "Victory or Death" and was addressed "To the People of Texas & All Americans in the World." The letter attracted fewer than one hundred men to the Alamo, but inspired others to join the Texas army and is considered a masterpiece of American patriotism.

On March 5, the night before the Alamo fell, Travis gathered his men and explained the Texians were vastly outnumbered. Legend holds that Travis drew a line in the dirt with his saber and asked those willing to die for the cause to cross and stand alongside him.

➡ **Do you know where your colleagues stand in your cause? What must you say or do to inspire your team when the odds are stacked overwhelmingly against you?**

The cannonade lasted until morning light.

At dawn, Santa Anna gave the order and more than two thousand Mexican soldiers stormed the Alamo.

Every defender—between 182 and 257 men—lost his life in a battle that lasted less than an hour.

Santa Anna reportedly told an officer the Battle of the Alamo "was but a small affair," who replied that "with another such victory as this, we'll go to the devil," having lost one-third of his army to win the battle.

As news of the Alamo's fall spread, residents fled on foot, fearing Santa Anna's wrath.

Susannah Dickinson was one of the noncombatants whose life was spared. Santa Anna forced her to identify the bodies and then reluctantly set her free. Every saga needs a storyteller, and Dickinson confirmed Travis gave his men the choice of escaping or staying to fight and die for the cause.

Santa Anna calculated the Alamo's fall would quell the resistance, but it had the opposite effect. Santa Anna's ruthless conduct and Travis's gallant leadership inspired volunteers, expanding the ranks of the young Texas army to more than fourteen hundred men.

General Sam Houston realized his small army of ill-trained men was capable of just one battle. Amid grumblings that he was a coward, Houston retreated 120 miles (193 km) toward the Louisiana border. On March 31, Houston camped at Groce's Landing on the Brazos River and began two weeks of rigorous military training.

Santa Anna, meanwhile, grew complacent and subdivided his troops.

"We view ourselves on the eve of battle," Sam Houston told his soldiers. "We are nerved for the conquest and must conquer or perish. It is vain to look for present aid: None is at hand. We must now act or abandon all hope!"

On April 21, Houston's army surprised Santa Anna's forces at the Battle of San Jacinto. With cries of "Remember the Alamo" ringing in their ears, Mexican troops were routed in a battle that lasted eighteen minutes.

Texas Independence—declared seven weeks earlier—was now a reality. Santa Anna's desire to win at all costs prompted this skilled soldier to ignore sound input and make bad decisions that eventually cost Mexico Texas. Sam Houston's decision to ignore grumblings brought Texas victory and independence.

➡ **As a leader, when do you listen to others and when do you ignore them?**

Remember your role! Remember the Alamo!

Franklin D. Roosevelt's "Hundred Days" Combats the Great Depression

How Urgent, Bold Action Saved America from Ruin

> "The country needs—and, unless I mistake its temper, the country demands—bold persistent experimentation. It is common sense to take a method and try it: If it fails, admit it frankly and try another. But above all, try something."
>
> **—FRANKLIN D. ROOSEVELT**

America was on her knees.

When the U.S. stock market crashed on October 29, 1929, "Black Tuesday" shock waves collapsed markets worldwide in an economic depression. By 1932, fifteen million Americans were out of work—one out of every three people. Capital investment dropped from \$10 billion in 1929 to \$1 billion in 1932. Farm income plummeted 60 percent.

Herbert Hoover was elected the United States' thirty-first president in 1929 on a platform of progressive business practices honed as the nation's third Secretary of Commerce. But when the bottom fell out six months after his inauguration, the harder Hoover worked to get America back on her feet, the worse things got.

Between 1929 and 1932, worldwide gross domestic product (GDP) fell by 15 percent. By comparison, worldwide GDP during the 2008–2009 Great Recession fell by less than one percent.

Voters would choose between Hoover and New York Governor Franklin D. Roosevelt as their president in November 1932 to save America from ruin.

When unemployed World War I veterans marched on Washington in July 1932 to petition Congress for early payment of a wartime bonus due in 1945, Hoover refused to meet with them. Recalling events of Russia's 1917 revolution, Hoover ordered White House gates padlocked. Though food, shelter, and medicine were provided, events turned tragic when police, ordered to move the "mob" from Pennsylvania Avenue, shot two veterans. Hoover ordered General Douglas MacArthur to disperse the "essence of revolution." Reading newspaper accounts of the incident, Roosevelt predicted, "MacArthur has just prevented Hoover's reelection."

By autumn, Americans had lost faith in their government, banks, and themselves.

Roosevelt campaigned on a "New Deal" for America. FDR was short on specifics, but his energy, charisma, and message of hope resonated. "Happy Days Are Here Again" played at all FDR events. Campaign manager Jim Farley observed that Roosevelt's "ability to discuss political issues in short, simple sentences made a powerful impression. There was a touch of destiny about the man."

Americans thought so, too, and elected FDR in a landslide.

⇒ **What's your inspiring vision for your organization? You can include financial targets, but your vision must give your colleagues something to cheer for.**

Until 1933, U.S. presidents elected in November took office in March. Hoover was a lame duck.

Fear flooded into the four-month void.

With no action from Hoover and FDR unwilling to lend Hoover support, Americans panicked, withdrawing gold and currency from banks. The day before FDR's inauguration, banks in thirty-two of the country's forty-eight states had closed. Deposits evaporated. Money was useless—there was nothing to buy.

For FDR's inauguration on Saturday, March 4, 1933, gloomy skies matched the nation's—and Hoover's—mood. FDR, fifty-one, radiated optimism.

In his address, FDR proclaimed he would speak with "candor," lead with "vigor," and act "boldly." He assured Americans of his "firm belief that the only thing we have to fear is fear itself." As he spoke, sunshine emerged.

While thousands attended inaugural celebrations, FDR invited his cabinet to the White House where Justice Benjamin Cardozo swore them in as a group—a first. Roosevelt had assembled his team in February, a bipartisan mix of conservatives and liberals, including the first female Secretary of Labor. FDR joked the Saturday swearing-in meant they would "receive an extra day's pay," but it signaled his presidency would start with action, not ceremony.

FDR stayed up past 1:00 a.m. discussing with longtime aide Louis Howe the plan that would become known as the "Hundred Days," the bold experiment in governing that set the bar for new leaders. Henceforth, the first hundred days for executives in all types of institutions would become the symbolic benchmark for measuring their early successes.

➡ **What bold action will you develop and lead to breathe new life into your organization?**

FDR's approach was informed by comments from three elder statesmen.

Antioch College professor Arthur Morgan inspired FDR to think big. Harvard president A. Lawrence Lowell encouraged FDR to take and hold the initiative with Congress. Retired Supreme Court justice Oliver Wendell Holmes told FDR, "You are in a war, Mr. President, and in a war there is only one rule, 'Form your battalion and fight!'"

On Sunday, March 5, 1933, FDR met with Congressional leaders to enlist their support, and then issued a proclamation closing the country's banks. FDR met with U.S. governors Monday to explain his decision; he received a standing ovation. Congress convened Thursday in a hundred-day special session. In just seven hours, legislation safeguarding banks and depositors was introduced, passed, and signed. FDR's first days in office set the tone for his presidency and were characterized by speed, confidence, and a willingness to try new things. "There are many ways of going forward," Roosevelt noted, "but only one way of standing still."

During the Hundred Days, FDR introduced and Congress established dozens of agencies that stimulated farm programs, initiated conservation programs, outlawed child labor, and lifted wages. Timing helped. With war looming, American industry awoke, providing new jobs and what Roosevelt called the "great arsenal of democracy."

FDR created opportunities to get Americans working and feeling good about themselves.

> ⟹ What will be your most significant leadership accomplishments during the next twelve months?

Though crippled by polio and unable to walk since age thirty-nine, FDR exhibited the courage, vision, and willpower to get America back on her feet.

John Adams Agrees to Defend British Soldiers Charged with Murder

How Facts and Integrity Brought Out the Best in People

> "Because power corrupts, society's demands for moral authority and character increase as the importance of the position increases."
>
> **—JOHN ADAMS**

When shots rang out and musket smoke cleared shortly after 9:00 p.m. on March 5, 1770, five men lay dead or dying on Boston's King Street.

The outbreak of the American Revolution was five years away, yet public sentiment was already running high against the British, and the "Boston Massacre" further heightened

American resentment against King George and his troops garrisoned in Boston.

Redcoats—four thousand of them—had been dispatched to Boston in 1768 following Parliament's decision to raise taxes yet again on the colonists, this time on purchases of tea, paper, paint, and glass. Boston was the capital of the Province of Massachusetts Bay with a population of twenty thousand, and its port enjoyed significant international trade. The town also was a hotbed of pre-Revolutionary rebellion.

Among those most vocal in their complaints against the British were silversmith Paul Revere and Samuel Adams, a failed merchant whose father offered him a partnership in his business supplying malt to nearby breweries.

On March 6, 1771, the day following the shooting, John Adams, Samuel's second cousin, was approached in his law office by James Forrest on behalf of British captain Thomas Preston, who had been arrested with his eight men earlier that day for the shooting. With more violence threatening, the British were intent on giving the soldiers a conspicuously fair trial.

All of the other American lawyers approached by Forrest had refused the case.

Adams, age thirty-four and contemplating public office, weighed the invitation from Forrest against the risk to his reputation, knowing his acceptance of the case meant he would be "incurring a clamor and popular suspicions and prejudices." As a patriot, Adams joined his countrymen in the outrage over the killings. As a lawyer, he believed all men were entitled to a fair trial.

Adams's integrity trumped his emotions, and he agreed to defend the British soldiers.

➡ **What's your approach to checking your emotions when making important decisions?**

Events proceeded briskly during the next two weeks.

The British agreed to withdraw their troops to Castle Island in Boston Harbor, and on March 8 the first four victims of the shooting were buried with great ceremony. When the fifth person died, he was buried alongside the others on March 17. Ten days later, Captain Preston and the eight soldiers were indicted for murder.

Two trials were set: Captain Preston's for October 24 and the enlisted soldiers' for November 27.

Meanwhile, Paul Revere fomented public opinion against the British with an engraving depicting Captain Preston ordering his soldiers to fire at point-blank range on a defenseless crowd.

But as Adams dug into the case, the facts emerged to tell a different story: British Private Hugh White was standing watch that evening near the Custom House when Edward Garrick, a wig-maker's apprentice, insulted a British captain. The captain ignored the taunt but White did not, and when Garrick continued his taunts, White hit Garrick on the side of his head with his musket, dropping Garrick to the ground.

Soon a crowd of fifty people had encircled White. Word reached Captain Preston who, deciding the greater risk was leaving White to fend for himself, ordered eight soldiers to accompany him to the scene.

By now the mob had grown and men were spitting on the soldiers and throwing snowballs, trash, and punches, daring the soldiers to open fire.

Tensions mounted, a scuffle ensued, and muskets were discharged.

It was now John Adams's moral obligation to follow the facts—wherever they led.

> ➡ To what extent do your personal issues color your view of performance—whether it's someone else's or yours?

As Captain Preston's trial began in Boston's hostile environment, passions were decidedly against him. At issue was whether he had given the order to fire.

Though John Adams's remarks are lost to posterity, the effectiveness of his defense is evident: Captain Preston was found "not guilty."

The second, longer trial of the eight soldiers opened on November 27. Adams called twenty-two witnesses. On December 3, Adams delivered his concluding defense of the soldiers, telling the jury it was the mob that incited the shooting, not the soldiers.

Adams reminded the jury that self-defense was a primary law of nature, and acting in self-defense is the only charge that could be proven against the soldiers. The deaths were regrettable, but "facts are stubborn things," Adams famously concluded, "and whatever may be our wishes, our inclinations, or the dictates of our passion, they cannot alter the state of facts and evidence."

The jury deliberated for two-and-a-half hours, returning to acquit six of the eight soldiers. The remaining two soldiers, though found guilty of manslaughter, were punished with only brands to their thumbs.

⇨ When performance expectations are clear and agreement
has been reached on measuring performance, the facts
speak for themselves. How consistently do you address
behavior that fails to match the expectations you've
established?

John Adams's decision to follow his moral compass and not his
emotions burnished his reputation—not only as an able lawyer,
but also as a man of great character. When one of Boston's legis-
lative seats opened three months later, Adams was the town's first
choice to fill the vacancy.

John Adams served as America's first vice president under
George Washington and later was elected the nation's second
president.

Abraham Lincoln's Shrewd Idea Exposes the South as the Aggressor

How Lincoln's Refusal to Accept Obvious Solutions Forced the South's Hand

> "Nearly all men can stand adversity, but if you want to test a man's character, give him power."
>
> **—ABRAHAM LINCOLN**

America's thirty-three states were united in name only.

The 1860 presidential election divided the country along philosophical and geographical lines, with agriculturally driven Southern states favoring states' rights (and slavery) and Northern industrial states supporting abolition.

Lincoln won the election with 40 percent of the vote, failing to win a single Southern state where, of those states' nine million people, four million were slaves.

Lincoln's Republican Party also was fractured. Seasoned politicians were incredulous at losing to a man with seemingly little commending him to the country's highest office. Lincoln had scant formal education, military experience, or diplomatic know-how. His executive competence was limited to running a two-man law office. He was a one-term congressman who twice failed to become a senator.

Yet this man of humble origins would become one of America's greatest presidents—second only to George Washington.

As election night turned to Wednesday morning, Lincoln listed his cabinet member choices. They were rivals—men who wanted to be president and who, after their appointments, continually coveted his job, often working to undermine their boss. Yet Lincoln invited these men to serve because he believed them to be "the very strongest men." He recognized the country demanded the best talent to address the inevitable war. He was fifty-one.

> ⇒ Great leaders aren't concerned with always being the smartest person in the room. How often and how well do you listen to others? What help do you need now? To whom will you turn?

Forty-four days after Lincoln's election, South Carolina became the first of seven states to secede. Southern militia began seizing federal courthouses, post offices, forts, and arsenals.

Major Robert Anderson, commander of Federal troops in Charleston Harbor, South Carolina, evaluated his position at

Fort Moultrie and found it wanting. The fort's twelve-foot walls afforded people standing on balconies of homes encircling the fort a threatening advantage. At midnight the night after Christmas, Anderson ordered Fort Moultrie's guns spiked, provisions burned, and the seventy-eight men and forty-five women and children evacuated to Fort Sumter.

President James Buchanan sent a ship to Fort Sumter with soldiers and supplies, but under Confederate artillery fire, the ship retreated. South Carolina Governor Francis Pickens then ordered President Buchanan to evacuate Fort Sumter. Buchanan's refusal left Anderson and his garrison stranded with dwindling supplies and incomplete defenses, surrounded by hostile forces.

On February 23, 1861, Lincoln snuck into Washington, DC, after threats on his life were discovered by his head of security, Allan Pinkerton.

Taking office the following month in one of the darkest hours in America's young existence, Lincoln resolved to preserve the Union. On his first day in office, Lincoln read Major Anderson's grim report: twenty-eight days' of provisions remained; mobilizing a military expedition would take months.

Lincoln convened his cabinet to weigh options. There seemed to be but two. If reinforcements were sent, Lincoln would break his promise that "the Government will not assail you" and the remaining Southern states likely would secede. Abandoning the fort would legitimize the Confederacy, and Lincoln's party might abandon him.

Fort Sumter was expendable militarily. Politically, it embodied the U.S. Constitution, which Lincoln had sworn to "preserve, protect, and defend."

Lincoln's cabinet was divided.

Despite relentless pressure, Lincoln remained outwardly calm and unwaveringly focused on preserving the Union. He punctuated tense situations with humor. Many cabinet members disapproved. "Gentlemen," asked Lincoln, "why don't you laugh? With the fearful strain that is upon me night and day, if I did not laugh I should die, and you need this medicine as much as I do."

> ➡ **How do you behave under pressure? How do you remain calm and clearheaded when leadership's burden is at its heaviest?**

The Lincolns' first state dinner was held March 28, honoring new cabinet members.

Before the dinner's end, Lincoln called his cabinet members aside and revealed General Winfield Scott's startling recommendation that Fort Sumter be evacuated. No decision was reached.

Lacking an acceptable solution, Lincoln roamed the White House at night unable to sleep. Migraine headaches incapacitated him. Lincoln, like Fort Sumter, was alone on an island. Time was running out. Yet Lincoln was insistent there must be a better solution than the two equally disastrous ones being considered. "I could not sleep," Lincoln recalled, "when I got on such a hunt after an idea, until I had caught it."

On March 29, Lincoln made a shrewd decision: he would alert South Carolina's governor of his plan to resupply Sumter. If the Southerners fired on an unarmed ship, they would be the aggressors. If not, the fort would be supplied.

Lincoln's cabinet approved the plan. Secret preparations began the next day. A government loan from New York money markets was scheduled for subscription on April 2; any visible preparations—either to reinforce or evacuate—would threaten the loan. Following the successful bond sale, Lincoln's plan was executed.

As Union ships sailed for Charleston Harbor, State Department clerk Robert Chew called on South Carolina Governor Pickens, reading a message composed by Lincoln and signed by the Secretary of War: the Governor was "to expect an attempt will be made to supply Fort Sumter with provisions only."

On April 11, the Confederates demanded the fort's surrender. Major Anderson declined.

On April 12 at 4:30 a.m., the Confederates fired the first shot of the Civil War.

➡ **How can you be sure you've considered every option to make the best possible decision?**

Abraham Lincoln guided the country through constitutional, military, and moral crises, preserving the Union, ending slavery, and promoting economic and financial modernization. All in just over four years.

The Final Days of America's Bloodiest Conflict Teach Us about Loss

How the Victors Showed Respect to the Vanquished as the Civil War Concluded

> "I leave comparisons to history, claiming only that I have acted in every instance from a conscientious desire to do what was right...failures have been errors of judgment, not of intent."
>
> **—ULYSSES S. GRANT**

On April 9, 1865, Union general Ulysses S. Grant accepted General Robert E. Lee's surrender of his Army of Northern Virginia at Appomattox Court House in Virginia, effectively ending the American Civil War.

The months and actions following Lincoln's 1864 reelection

signaled the end for the South and showcased the character of
leaders on both sides as they dealt with victory and loss.

In February 1865, Lincoln rejected Confederate president
Jefferson Davis's request for peace because Davis wanted the
South to remain independent. The following month, retreating Confederates burned Richmond, Virginia, to prevent Union
troops from capturing it. By early April, Lee's retreating army was
exhausted, outnumbered, and out of options.

Believing the end was near, Grant wrote to Lee: "The result
of the last week must convince you of the hopelessness of further
resistance."

Lee wanted one more chance for his army to escape. When it
became clear he was surrounded on three sides, Lee realized the
war was over and he agreed to surrender.

> ⇨ **One of your toughest decisions is assessing correctly
> the performance gap—real or imagined—that exists
> between your organization and its customers and suppli-
> ers or between two colleagues. Your assessment will help
> answer a difficult question: How much more time will we
> invest in this cause?**

The Civil War was America's bloodiest conflict.

More than 620,000 soldiers died, 476,000 were wounded,
another 400,000 missing. By the war's end, "our bleeding,
bankrupt, almost dying country also longs for peace," wrote
journalist Horace Greeley.

Once Lee accepted the inevitability that surrender was
imminent, he wrote to Grant requesting terms. The eight letters

Grant and Lee exchanged leading to their meeting at Appomattox Court House offer insight to each man's character.

Grant stipulated that officers give their word that they would not take up arms against their country. Officers were allowed to keep their pistols and sabers, and the defeated Confederates were allowed to return home with their horses and mules.

The terms were as generous as Lee could hope for since his men would not be imprisoned nor prosecuted for treason.

"The friend in my adversity I shall always cherish most," said Grant. "I can better trust those who helped to relieve the gloom of my dark hours than those who are so ready to enjoy with me the sunshine of my prosperity."

Performance is a choice. The person or organization unable or unwilling to perform has made a choice and must be prepared to accept the consequences of that decision. Your responsibility as the leader is ensuring the rewards and penalties for performance are reasonable and clear, and executed consistently and fairly.

> ➡ **Have you done everything in your power to save this rela-
> tionship, or is there something else you can do that you've
> not yet tried? What's preventing you from making one
> last attempt? What's the best possible outcome to strive
> for in this challenging relationship?**

Grant received Lee's letter inquiring about the terms of surrender on the morning of April 9, 1865, and his reply that Lee determine "where you wish the interview [i.e., meeting] to take place" is remarkable because it allowed the defeated Lee to choose the place of his surrender.

Grant's generous offer allowing the Confederates to keep their horses and mules meant spring planting could proceed. Grant also provided Lee with food rations for twenty-five thousand men, which Lee said would "do much toward reconciling the country."

The character of Lee and Grant was of such a high order that the surrender at Appomattox has been called "The Gentlemen's Agreement." With surrender papers signed, Lee rode away and Grant's men began cheering in celebration. Grant ordered an immediate stop to the cheering, saying, "The Confederates were now our countrymen, and we did not want to exult over their downfall."

Three days later, Union brigadier general Joshua L. Chamberlain led a formal surrender ceremony, and later wrote a moving tribute:

> The momentous meaning of this occasion impressed me deeply. I resolved to mark it by...a salute of arms. Before us in proud humiliation stood the embodiment of manhood: men whom neither toils and sufferings, nor the fact of death, nor disaster, nor hopelessness could bend from their resolve; standing before us now, thin, worn, and famished, but erect, and with eyes looking level into ours, waking memories that bound us together as no other bond;— was not such manhood to be welcomed back into a Union so tested and assured? Instructions had been given...and instantly our whole line...gives the soldier's salutation.... [Confederate general John Brown] Gordon at the head of the column, riding with heavy spirit and downcast face, catches the sound of shifting arms, looks up, and, taking

the meaning, wheels superbly, making with himself and his horse one uplifted figure, with profound salutation as he drops the point of his sword to the boot toe; then facing to his own command, gives word for his successive brigades to pass us with the same position of the manual—honor answering honor.

> ⮕ How do you plan to communicate the termination of the relationship internally and externally?

Conduct final meetings in a professional and respectful manner. It's the right thing to do. And you never know when your paths will cross again.

Apollo 13's Mid-Flight Explosion Threatens Crew's Safe Return to Earth

How Impossible Deadlines and Improvisation Turned Catastrophe into Triumph

> "There is no such thing as good enough. You, your team, and your equipment must be the best. That is how you win victories."
>
> **—GENE KRANZ**

Russian cosmonaut Yuri Gagarin became the first human in space on April 12, 1961.

World leadership was now measured by space leadership. America was behind.

Answers to President John F. Kennedy's pointed questions

indicated Russia could be beaten, but America would have to play serious catch-up, having "failed to make the necessary hard decisions" declaring space exploration a priority.

Six weeks after Gagarin's orbit, Kennedy told Congress that "landing a man on the moon and returning him safely to the earth" was America's new goal. Kennedy wanted the goal achieved "before this decade is out." Kennedy wasn't that interested in space, but the idea of Russian technological, military, and ideological supremacy was a Cold War threat to America. And, perhaps just as importantly, an embarrassment.

On July 20, 1969, the world watched Neil Armstrong and Buzz Aldrin step onto the moon's surface, plant the American flag, and rejoin fellow astronaut Michael Collins for *Apollo 11's* safe return home.

America had won the Space Race and made it look easy.

Most people didn't fully appreciate the risks. Astronaut Ted Freeman died in 1964 ejecting from his aircraft. Neil Armstrong— the first man on the moon—and Dave Scott nearly died in 1966 when their *Gemini 8* thrusters malfunctioned. In the Apollo program's early days, thousands of systems failures plagued the spacecraft that would hurl men toward the moon. Following one prototype inspection, Gus Grissom—who would die with fellow astronauts Ed White and Roger Chaffee in a launch pad fire in 1967—placed a lemon atop the command module.

After *Apollo 11*, space flight lost its luster. *Apollo 13's* April 11, 1970, launch was overshadowed by Paul McCartney's disclosure he was leaving The Beatles, and by updates from Vietnam, where American casualties reached an eleven-month high.

Apollo 8's Christmas Eve live broadcast in 1968 was the

most-watched television broadcast; coverage of *Apollo 11*'s 1969 moon landing eclipsed those ratings. Now *Apollo 13* commander Jim Lovell (a participant in *Apollo 8*'s broadcast) was sending greetings from space to a mostly empty room at NASA.

Six minutes later, following Mission Control's routine request to stir *Apollo 13*'s oxygen and hydrogen tanks, warnings flashed aboard the spacecraft and back home. Something was terribly wrong.

> ➡ **How often are you surprised when bad things happen?**
> **What patterns have you ignored?**

"It looks to me," Lovell reported to Mission Control as he peered through a port, "that we are venting something."

"OK," said Flight Director Gene Kranz, "let's everybody keep cool. Let's solve the problem, but let's not make it any worse by guessing."

In the crippled dual-module spacecraft—the Command Module (CM), *Odyssey*, attached by a sealed tunnel to the Lunar Excursion Module (LEM), *Aquarius*—the astronauts weren't guessing. There would be no moon landing. At fifty-five hours, fifty-four minutes, and fifty-three seconds into the mission, 200,000 miles (321,869 km) from Earth, moving at 25,000 miles per hour (40,234 km per hour), *Apollo 13* had lost half its oxygen supply and half its power.

Lovell did the math and knew a safe return to Earth would take one hundred hours. *Odyssey* had five hours of oxygen remaining. *Aquarius* had forty-five hours remaining. "If we're going to get home," Lovell informed Fred Haise and Jack Swigert, "we're going to have to use *Aquarius*."

In 1959, Gene Kranz helped write the policy for conducting a manned space flight, giving the flight director unquestioned authority "for the safety of the crew and the conduct of the flight regardless of the mission rules."

Kranz's April 13, 1970, directive to shut down *Apollo 13*'s fuel cell three to preserve power made it official: mission aborted. The pilots and scientists had laughed off superstitions with the number 13. Now Kranz had to get *Apollo 13* home.

America was in danger of losing its first manned space flight.

> ➡ **Who has the real authority in your business to say yes and no? Who has the influence?**

When media placed the odds of *Apollo 13*'s safe return at 10 percent, a previously indifferent world became riveted to this celestial drama.

Ingenious problem-solving, gutsy decision-making, and precise execution under near-impossible time constraints brought the astronauts safely home. Five huge problems topped the list.

First, Mission Control vetoed a direct return, which, though quicker, would consume lots of fuel; *Apollo 13* would leverage the moon's gravitational pull to slingshot itself back to Earth.

Second, the LEM was designed for two people for thirty-six hours, not three people for four days. To maintain life-support and communication systems until reentry, engineers calculated powering down the LEM to its lowest levels.

Third, carbon dioxide emitted by the astronauts would poison them. The CM had enough canisters, but they were incompatible with those in the LEM. Engineers improvised a solution, joining cube-shaped CM canisters to the LEM's cylindrical canister-sockets with a duct taped–wrapped hose.

Fourth, powering the CM back up required a new procedure not contemplated (much less accomplished) in a cabin where temperatures hovered at 39°F (4°C).

Fifth, the Service Module (SM) and LEM had to be jettisoned before reentry. Six engineers had six hours to solve this problem.

Each crisis was averted, each obstacle overcome.

As *Apollo 13* splashed down safely in the South Pacific Ocean, the world celebrated.

⇒ **What challenge appears unsolvable? A solution exists. What is it?**

Apollo 13's failed lunar mission would come to be regarded by many as NASA's finest hour.

Winston Churchill Gives the Worst Speech of His Life

How a Speech You've Never Heard of Became a Great Orator's Most Important Delivery

> "Continuous effort—not strength or intelligence—is the key to unlocking our potential."
>
> **—WINSTON CHURCHILL**

Winston Churchill's Maiden Speech to the House of Commons—delivered February 18, 1901, at age twenty-six—"held a crowded House spellbound," declared London's *Daily Express*.

Perhaps he was given the benefit of the doubt.

His father, Lord Randolph Churchill, was a brilliant speaker known for his quick mind and sharp tongue. Young Winston, however, was not a natural speaker. Churchill possessed a slight lisp and consulted a noted specialist, whose initial advice was "practice and perseverance." Extra effort would be required.

Churchill knew public speaking held the key to his unbridled ambitions. His 1897 essay, "The Scaffolding of Rhetoric," declared, "Of all the talents bestowed upon men, none is so precious as the gift of oratory."

For Churchill, words mattered, noting "the shorter words of a language…appeal with greater force to simple understanding," polishing his idea years later into a pithier gem: "The short words are the best, and the old words best of all."

Churchill even memorized his speeches, prompting some to say his delivery lacked "veracity."

Now, three years after his debut, Churchill stood at a pivotal point: should he cross the floor from the conservative Tory bench to join the Liberals? Churchill's isolation grew as Conservatives shunned him and Liberals remained wary.

Churchill landed a few blows against conservative policies, but some took exception to his approach. "Is it really necessary," Joseph Chamberlain wrote to him, "to be quite as personal in your speeches?"

On April 22, 1904, Churchill rose in the House of Commons to deliver a speech supporting the Trade Unions and Trade Disputes Bill. This otherwise forgettable speech is historic because of its catastrophic conclusion and Churchill's decision in its aftermath.

At the forty-five-minute mark, Churchill forgot what came next. He stopped, stammered, and sat down. Those with vivid memories of his father's deterioration before his death at forty-five were "aghast," concerned Winston had inherited his father's illness. "Mr. Churchill Breaks Down," cried newspapers. He received letters, urging him not to "over-exert yourself in your unceasing devotion to the service of the country."

Churchill knew better. Pronouncing his effort a "complete disaster," he vowed he'd never deliver another speech without better preparation and a complete set of notes in hand. "Winston," said his friend F. E. Smith, "has spent the best years of his life composing his impromptu speeches."

⇒ How determined are you to work for your success? Are you setting individual and organizational performance bars high enough? What would 10 percent more effort produce?

"Politics," said Churchill, "is almost as exciting as war, and quite as dangerous. In war, you can only be killed once, but in politics many times."

Churchill was in and out of favor regularly. In May 1935, he was alone in his warnings of Adolf Hitler:

When the situation was manageable it was neglected, and now that it is thoroughly out of hand we apply too late the remedies which then might have effected a cure. There is nothing new in the story…Want of foresight, unwillingness to act when action would be simple and effective, lack of clear thinking, confusion of counsel until the emergency comes, until self-preservation strikes its jarring gong.

By May 1940, Neville Chamberlain's leadership had failed Britain; Churchill was appointed Prime Minister. "You have an enormous task," W. H. Thompson told Churchill on the drive back from Buckingham Palace.

Churchill's first task was extricating 340,000 soldiers pinned against the sea at Dunkirk. Some British leaders considered surrendering to Germany. Churchill rallied his countrymen to achieve a miraculous rescue.

Tell the truth to the British people, Churchill counseled, as "they are the only people who like to be told how bad things are, who like to be told the worst."

> ➡ **What's your communication style? How can you ensure that what you're saying is being received the way you intend?**

Having overcome a speech impediment and political abandonment, Churchill, in the words of journalist Edward R. Murrow, "mobilized the English language and sent it into battle."

His first public address as Prime Minister made clear his vision for the British nation:

I have nothing to offer but blood, toil, tears, and sweat. We have before us an ordeal of the most grievous kind. We have before us many, many months of struggle and suffering.

You ask, what is our policy? I can say: It is to wage war by land, sea, and air, with all our might and with all the strength that God can give us; to wage war against a monstrous tyranny, never surpassed in the dark, lamentable catalogue of human crime. That is our policy.

You ask, what is our aim? I can answer in one word: It is victory, victory at all costs, victory in spite of all terrors, victory, however long and hard the road may be; for without victory, there is no survival.

Words—whether read by the eye or heard by the ear—are tools leaders use to console, educate, influence, and inspire.

> ➡ **If you had to leave your organization for a year and the only communication allowed was a single paragraph, what would you write?**

Churchill received the Nobel Prize in 1953 "for his mastery of historical and biographical description" and "brilliant oratory in defending exalted human values."

Barack Obama Deploys SEAL Team 6 on Operation Neptune Spear

How Relentless Pursuit and a Gutsy Decision Brought the World's Most Wanted Man to Justice

> "If we have Osama bin Laden in our sights and the Pakistani government is unable or unwilling to take them out, then I think that we have to act, and we will take them out. We will kill bin Laden. We will crush al-Qaeda. That has to be our biggest national security priority."
>
> **—BARACK OBAMA**

The world's most wanted man had vanished.

Osama bin Laden—privileged son of a wealthy Saudi family, founder of al-Qaeda, architect of the September 11 attacks on America—was on the run after vaulting to the top of the FBI's Most Wanted Fugitives List with a $25 million bounty on his head.

The U.S. intelligence community had monitored bin Laden's activities since his founding of al-Qaeda in 1988. Following al-Qaeda's August 7, 1998, embassy bombings in Africa, President Bill Clinton signed orders to capture or kill bin Laden. Thirteen days later, missiles obliterated a terrorist training camp, missing bin Laden by hours. Other missions were prepared; all failed or were aborted.

By December 1998, intelligence reports indicated al-Qaeda planned to attack America. Hijacked aircraft were said to play a role.

As George Bush succeeded Bill Clinton as president in January 2000, al-Qaeda's activity was spiking.

By September 2001, al-Qaeda's terrorist plot had succeeded. Bin Laden fled to the hills of Afghanistan and was tracked to the caves of Tora Bora. An eleven-day battle ensued; once again bin Laden escaped.

His trail went cold. For the next eight years, bin Laden hid as America expended vast amounts of resources confronting terror in Iraq and Afghanistan.

President Barack Obama succeeded Bush, and in May 2009 made the hunt for bin Laden his administration's top national security priority. Under Bush, fighting terrorism had weakened al-Qaeda but the focus on bin Laden had blurred. Obama demanded weekly progress reports from CIA Director Leon Panetta, heightening focus and urgency.

> ➡ **To what priorities are you most committed? When comparing your priorities to an objective assessment of performance, what do you see?**

By early 2011, methodical work pursuing leads and connecting dots led the intelligence team tracking bin Laden to a compound in Abbottabad, Pakistan.

As steps were taken to confirm bin Laden's presence, two options emerged: bombing the compound versus deploying a small, highly trained military unit.

Admiral William McRaven, commander of the Joint Special Operations Command, was told to assemble a team.

The SEALs—Sea, Air, Land teams—trace their beginnings to World War II when covert reconnaissance of landing beaches intensified. Over time, the teams evolved to include the demolition of enemy landing defenses and, ultimately, to commando-type raids. An early SEAL team member describing their work said, "We were ready to do what nobody else could do, and what nobody else wanted to do."

To become a SEAL, technical skills and physical ability meet the highest standards of excellence. "And perhaps above all, your character is under a microscope at all times," says Navy SEAL Marcus Luttrell. "Instructors, teachers, senior chiefs, and officers are always watching for the character flaw, the weakness which may one day lead to the compromise of your teammates. We can't stand that. We can stand damn near anything, except that."

As you assess your colleagues' character, consider, too, whether your organization's structure gives some people a hiding place.

During the punishing training all candidates must survive to become a Navy SEAL, the "Gray Man" is "the guy who blended into the group. Never the best guy, but also not the worst, the Gray Man always met the standards, exceeding them rarely, and stayed invisible," writes Mark Owen, a pseudonym for a former Navy SEAL.

➡ **How should your organization be structured to get the best results? Is there a "Gray Man" on your team?**

Obama pressed for better evidence.

Only operatives on the ground could pursue the intel Obama wanted. The likelihood of securing new information was infinitesimal; the odds of calling attention to the people asking questions was high and risked compromising the mission.

At the end of March, McRaven had developed a plan for how the attack would be carried out if SEALs were deployed. April 7 dress rehearsals carried out on a full-size model compound were reviewed by military brass. Operational confidence was high.

The key question: was the man in the compound bin Laden or someone else? There was no additional intel.

Leaders must learn to deal with probabilities. "No issue comes to my desk that is perfectly solvable," Obama recalled. "Because if people were absolutely certain then it would have been decided by somebody else."

On April 28, Obama assembled his team and polled them one by one. There was clear support to deploy the SEALs, but no consensus. The next morning, Obama gave the word: "It's a go."

On a moonless night on Monday, May 1, two helicopters lifted off at 11:00 p.m. local time carrying SEALs for the ninety-minute flight to the Abbottabad compound.

By the early morning hours of May 2, the world's most wanted man had been brought to justice.

> ➡ Are you making decisions only you can make? How often do decisions reach you that should be made by others?

"This conflict was begun on the timing and terms of others," said President Bush at a church service three days after the 9/11 attacks. "It will end in a way and at an hour of our choosing."

President Obama's decision set in motion the events that fulfilled the promise made nearly ten years earlier.

Mona Lisa Is Sold to the King of France

How a Masterpiece Was Monetized

> "Where the spirit does not work with the hand, there is no art."
>
> **—LEONARDO DA VINCI**

On May 9, 1517, Cardinal Luigi d'Aragona and his entourage departed on a "Grand Tour" that would lead them to the world's most famous painting.

By October 1517, the Cardinal had arranged an audience with Leonardo da Vinci in what is now Clos Lucé near Amboise, France. During this visit, da Vinci's masterpiece—the *Mona Lisa*—was shown for the first time.

What was it about this painting that caused a sensation at the time, and how did it become the world's most widely known image? Da Vinci left few clues about his painting, but his work offers traces of insights for those who aspire to make their organization a masterpiece.

Mystery has contributed to the *Mona Lisa*'s fame. Is the painting of Lisa, the wife of wealthy silk merchant Francesco del Giocondo? Or is the enigmatic woman a mistress of Giuliano de' Medici? And if the painting now in Paris's Louvre is the one commissioned by Medici, what happened to the portrait of del Giocondo's wife?

Whatever theory you accept, it's clear that by 1500, da Vinci's reputation was secured. The *Mona Lisa* is his crowning achievement in a life marked by breakthroughs in sculpting, science, architecture, anatomy, botany, mathematics, engineering, and geology.

How did da Vinci earn his reputation?

Around 1475, when Leonardo was twenty-three years old, his work as the pupil of Andrea del Verrocchio on the *Baptism of Christ* prompted people to take note.

Young Leonardo's insatiably curious mind, acute eye for detail, and dexterity with pencil and brush were evident in his work. Commissions followed, and he soon found favor with Italy's powerful Medici family.

Da Vinci's interest in anatomy contributed to his talent as a sculptor. His 1490 drawing of the *Vitruvian Man* is one of the world's most reproduced icons.

Da Vinci's passion for facts, figures, and logic separated him from his contemporaries. His mathematical, engineering, and drawing skills gained him employment as a military architect, engineer, and mapmaker.

As he continued to paint, da Vinci's reputation grew. His fresco *The Last Supper*, completed in 1495, is the world's single-most reproduced religious image.

While da Vinci is usually considered, along with Michelangelo and Raphael, as one of the three giants of the Italian Renaissance, Leonardo was twenty-three years old when Michelangelo was born and thirty-one when Raphael was born. Da Vinci paved the way.

Staking your claim in people's hearts and minds means owning a single word. For Apple, it's "think"; for Google, it's "search." For Leonardo da Vinci, it's two words: "Renaissance Man."

⟶ **What one word do you want to own in the minds of your employees, customers, and partners?**

The first written reference to the *Mona Lisa* appears in the diary of Antonio de Beatis, who was among Cardinal Luigi's entourage.

In the October 10, 1517, entry in his travel journal, de Beatis writes that visitors were shown three paintings by da Vinci: one of the Madonna and Child in the lap of St. Anne, one of a young St. John the Baptist, and a third painting that turned out to be da Vinci's masterpiece, the *Mona Lisa*.

The visitors were struck immediately by the *Mona Lisa*'s beauty and also by its originality: no subject had ever been painted with a smile.

Da Vinci used a shadowing technique called *sfumato* that blurred the images of his subjects, allowing them to meld with the surrounding landscape to create an ethereal subtlety that had never before been achieved.

Da Vinci's misty background with aerial views and a landscape—muted in contrast to the vibrancy of the lifelike appearance of this enigmatic woman—was remarkable in that it showed no visible brushstrokes.

The *Mona Lisa* was at once beautiful and original.

> ➡ **Da Vinci's inventive mind was comfortable experimenting with new ideas. What's your view of taking a risk and trying something new?**

It's unclear why da Vinci never presented the painting to del Giocondo.

Some historians believe da Vinci considered it his favorite and refused to part with it.

Other scholars point to the hundreds of unfinished works da Vinci left behind and believe he was still working on the painting at the time of his death.

We know for certain that upon da Vinci's death on May 2, 1519, at age sixty-seven, the artist's longtime assistant Gian Giacomo Caprotti da Oreno, better known as Salaì, inherited the work and sold it to France's King Francis I for 4,000 gold crowns.

Though commissioned in Italy, this masterpiece today is the property of the French Republic and hangs in the Louvre. When I viewed it, I was surprised by its small size: 20.87 inches wide (53 centimeters) by 30.32 inches high (77 centimeters).

Its value is estimated at $800 million.

The *Mona Lisa* is a beautiful painting. Da Vinci's reputation contributes to its value. If someone else had painted it, would it still be as valuable?

➡ **What is the value of the masterpiece you're creating? How much money do you require to be happy in retirement? Do your loved ones agree?**

What will it take for you to create a *Mona Lisa*?

Hattie Caraway Becomes First Woman Elected to the U.S. Senate

How Double Standards Made a Tough Job Tougher

> "My idea of the job is to do my level best to represent the people of my state."
>
> **—HATTIE CARAWAY**

When U.S. senator Thad Caraway died on November 6, 1931, his wife was invited to take his seat.

Several factors influenced the Arkansas Democratic leaders' decision.

It was the law. If Thad Caraway had lived three days longer, Arkansas governor Harvey Parnell could have appointed a person of his choosing. Arkansas law stipulated a special election was required.

It was practical. With the special election sixty-six days away and holidays approaching, party leaders didn't have enough time to determine another candidate.

It was a courtesy. In addition to being an honor, it was known Hattie needed the income while she planned her future.

There was another factor: Hattie was not considered a long-term solution because she was a woman.

The following week, the *Jonesboro Evening Appeal* reported that Hattie "would agree to accept the nomination...if it is offered to her." The article noted, "Although she made no statement regarding the matter, leaders were confident that Mrs. Caraway would not seek to succeed herself in the next general election."

Party leaders underestimated Hattie Caraway.

> ➡ **Who are you underestimating? Who—given the opportunity and some encouragement—might surprise you?**

As expected, Hattie Caraway won the special election, becoming the first woman elected as a U.S. senator.

Hattie took the job seriously. She arrived in Washington, DC, with more qualifications than most women of her era. She was a college graduate, she had managed her family's small cotton plantation in her husband's absence, and she deployed a common-sense approach to her work.

It wasn't easy. As the first woman in the ultimate boys club, Hattie had no mentors and no confidants. While she was virtually ignored by fellow Arkansas senator Joe T. Robinson, she knew that any errant step by her would be magnified. Hattie paid attention, spoke little, and developed new skills.

She arrived in her office every day at 8:00 a.m. where she

first read the *Congressional Record* and studied bills. She rarely made speeches in the Senate, recognizing her raised voice (there were no microphones) would sound strident. Hattie chose to exert her influence in the small but powerful committees on which she served.

Her leadership style was authentic, noting in her journal, "And they say women talk all the time. There's been a lot of 'old woman's talk' here tonight—but I haven't done any of it."

But on May 9, 1932, Hattie spoke. She had made the biggest decision of her life.

Hattie announced she would seek a second term in the Senate. She was fifty-four. In her journal, Hattie wrote, "If the people of my State continue me here, I shall not regret the long hours, nor the mental strain… My, I feel so alone—so bad indeed—but I shall hold on to my courage."

For the 1932 Senate race, Hattie faced six other candidates—all men. All formidable.

Running on her record, and aided on the campaign trail by Louisiana politician Huey Long and on the ballot by Franklin D. Roosevelt, Hattie received more votes than the other six candidates combined.

She made history as she returned to the U.S. Senate for another term.

> ⇒ **In what areas do you need to develop to become a more effective leader?**

Hattie's legacy of legislation remains significant.

She sponsored legislation to provide training and education for returning war veterans (the GI Bill); create a peacekeeping organization that became the United Nations; and develop millions of dollars' worth of projects for education, flood control, agriculture, and forestry.

Grace Stinnett Bustin, my grandmother, was born twenty-one years after Hattie. She became an elected statewide leader of the Parent Teacher Association, beginning in 1933—one year after Hattie took office.

A document in my grandmother's files that was typed on her typewriter articulates the difficult role any leader faces...especially female leaders.

"The Leader's Easy Job"

Her job is something like a football in a big game;
First one side has it and then the other:
If she writes a postal, it is too short,
If she sends a letter, it's too long,
If she issues a pamphlet, she is a spendthrift.
If she attempts to safeguard the interests of the association, she is
*   trying to run things,*
If she does not, she is allowing things to go to the dogs.
If she attends committee meetings, she is intruding,
If she does not, she is a shirker.
If the attendance is slim—well, nobody likes her anyway.
If she tries to help, she is a pest.
If the program is a success, the program committee is praised,
If not, it's all the president's fault.

If dues are called for, she is insulting,
If they are not collected, she is to blame.
If she is in a smiling mood, she is frivolous,
If she is serious, she is a sorehead.
If she seeks advice, she is incompetent,
If she does not, she is bullheaded.
If she mixes with the members, she is too familiar,
If she does not, she is too ritzy.
So, ashes to ashes, dust to dust,
If others won't do it, the president must.

Leadership is hard work. It's not doing what's easy or popular. It's doing what's right and necessary.

➡ **What's your leadership philosophy? List the best and worst traits of leaders you've known. What top three or four characteristics do you want to be known for? Now articulate your philosophy.**

For better or worse, the organization you lead reflects your leadership style.

Charles Dow Develops a Stock-Picking Index in Use More Than a Century Later

How Seeing an Unmet Need Produced a System That Changed the American Stock Market

> "The present is always tending toward the future and there are always in existing conditions signals of danger or encouragement for those who read with care."
>
> **—CHARLES DOW**

Some people believe the stock market is legalized gambling.

But unlike games of chance where luck determines winners, playing the stock market is betting on a company's leaders to produce sustainable value.

Following the War of 1812, America's western expansion

attracted developers and speculators. Government bonds were sold to fund improvements. New York City benefited from the opening of the Erie Canal, the only eastern seaport providing inland waterways. In 1865, the New York Stock Exchange—founded in 1792—expanded to support investors betting on public projects and private companies. Investors' need for financial updates intensified, so firms capable of providing accurate information quickly flourished as glorified messenger services.

Charles Dow thrived as a business reporter, learning his craft in Providence, Rhode Island, from Samuel Bowles, who instructed his protégés when writing news stories to "put it all in the first sentence." Reporting suited Dow. He was economical with words—spoken and written. Opportunities to interview successful financiers enabled Dow to learn the type of information investors craved. Investors appreciated Dow's accuracy, integrity, and confidentiality.

New York had emerged as America's financial center, so Dow left Providence in 1880, finding work at the Kiernan Wall Street Financial News Bureau.

Dow persuaded John J. Kiernan to hire his friend Edward Jones, who was a whiz at dissecting financial reports. Dow and Jones were scrupulously honest, refusing bribes to slant reports to increase a company's stock price. Dow and Jones also shared a growing frustration as Kiernan ignored or rebuffed their suggestions to offer new services. Dow and Jones had plenty of ideas and, thwarted by Kiernan, discussed starting their own firm. But they had little money.

A third Kiernan employee—Charles Bergstresser— developed a mechanism that quadrupled printing productivity.

When Kiernan refused to give Bergstresser equity for his invention, Bergstresser helped fund Dow and Jones's new venture.

In November 1882, Dow, Jones & Company was established at 15 Wall Street in a small, unpainted basement.

> ⇒ **How do your colleagues greet change? Are new initiatives received enthusiastically or resisted?**

Observation. Curiosity. Intelligence. Urgency. Discipline.

Taken alone, these behaviors get you only so far. Together, they can generate something powerful. Dow, Jones, and Bergstresser possessed these qualities, with each bringing a particular strength that helped the young company distinguish itself from other news-gathering firms.

In addition to financing the venture, Charles Bergstresser, twenty-four, was known for getting tight-lipped financiers like J. P. Morgan to share news. Bergstresser's skills enabled the firm to secure hard-to-come-by interviews.

Edward Jones, twenty-six, had a nose for news. He was regarded as Wall Street's first analyst and was an accomplished editor. Jones became a regular at the Windsor Hotel—called "All-Night Wall Street"—socializing with financiers and obtaining information. Jones also directed daily operations.

Charles Dow, thirty-one, was an introvert whose financial reporting featured crisp writing with compelling insights unearthed through deep research. "Mr. Dow could make more out of a single sentence or a single fact than anyone I knew," said his successor Thomas F. Woodlock.

Dow believed investors would welcome an expanded news

report, and a *Customers' Afternoon Letter* debuted in November 1883. Written chiefly by Dow, this two-page report summarized each day's trading and occasionally forecasted upcoming financial developments. Circulation soon swelled to one thousand subscriptions.

New York, besides being a port city, was served by twenty railroads. Updates concerning these companies interested investors. On July 3, 1884, Dow, Jones & Company published the average closing prices of representative active stocks—originally, ten railroad and two industrial companies.

Five years later, having grown to fifty employees, the partners converted the two-page "flimsies" into the *Wall Street Journal.* The first edition debuted on July 8, 1889, with delivery of the Dow Jones News Service via telegraph.

But of all the *Journal's* innovations, the biggest by far was the Dow Jones Industrial Average.

In 1896, Charles Dow evaluated current market conditions and believed the time had come to create an index featuring industrial stocks. While industrial companies were emerging, major railroad companies dominated investor interest since they were viewed as America's economic growth engines.

On May 26, 1896, Dow calculated the average of twelve stocks and published the Dow Jones Industrial Average, the first of several indices of stocks and prices on the New York Stock Exchange. It was a bold move.

⇒ **What are your customers' unmet needs?**

"We publish what the bond houses and the traders say they want," the *Journal* trumpeted.

What the paper's constituency wanted was summarized in what today we'd call a mission statement: "Its object is to give fully and fairly the daily news attending the fluctuations in prices of stocks, bonds, and some classes of commodities. It will aim steadily at being a paper of news and not a paper of opinions."

Dow, Jones, and Bergstresser promised to publish a paper that would not be controlled by advertisers, and the *Journal* published names of companies that withheld information about profit and loss, earning the respect of its readers.

➡ **How does your organization measure value? To what extent do your people understand how to create and optimize it?**

The *Journal*, printed continuously since its inception, is the world's largest daily newspaper, with a circulation of more than two million. Investors continue to rely on the Dow Jones Industrial Average.

Max Lauffer Invites Jonas Salk to Establish His Lab at the University of Pittsburgh

How Lauffer's Gamble and Salk's Work Combined to Cure the World's Worst Epidemic

"I have had dreams and I have had nightmares, but I have conquered my nightmares because of my dreams."

—JONAS SALK

Not since the bubonic plague had an epidemic decimated, mystified, and terrified humankind.

From 1347 to 1351, the Black Death killed two hundred million people, between 30 to 60 percent of the planet's population. It would take two hundred years for the world to recover.

At the turn of the twentieth century, poliomyelitis was

infecting mankind. Poliomyelitis, or polio, entered the body as a virus, assaulting nerve cells in the bloodstream, causing headaches, fever, and vomiting. Within days, those stricken were paralyzed or dead. In 1789, English physician Michael Underwood identified polio as a distinct illness. In 1908, Austrian physicians Karl Landsteiner and Erwin Popper pinpointed the virus.

But it's one thing to understand polio and quite another to treat it.

In 1919, polio killed 850,000 Americans and more than twenty million people worldwide. Millions more were disabled. Polio was now one of the world's most feared diseases.

Thirty-six years would pass before a cure was discovered.

➡ **What must you do to ensure your organization is changing as fast as the world around you?**

As polio attacked the world, Franklin D. Roosevelt became its most famous victim.

He'd contracted the virus on August 11, 1921, and was luckier than most. He didn't die. He was paralyzed from the chest down.

Five years later, Roosevelt purchased a "four-story firetrap" in Warm Springs, Georgia, establishing a resort and clinic for polio victims. Two years later, FDR became New York's governor, and by November 1932 he'd become America's president. Roosevelt never allowed himself to be photographed in a wheelchair, yet he used his position "to make America 'polio conscious,'" calling his efforts a "crusade."

With the slogan "Dance so that others might walk," fund-raising galas were held nationwide on January 30, 1934, FDR's birthday, raising more than $1 million for polio research. FDR founded a foundation in 1937, and Broadway star Eddie Cantor became an early volunteer, coining the name March of Dimes, which later became the foundation's name. When Cantor urged Americans to send their dimes to FDR for his birthday, thousands of letters containing dimes flooded the White House. To commemorate FDR's leadership, the Roosevelt dime was created after his death in 1945 and issued in 1946 on what would have been his sixty-fourth birthday.

The same year FDR held his first fund-raising gala, the man who eventually would use those funds to cure polio completed his undergraduate studies.

Jonas Salk planned to study law in college but was overruled by his mother. Salk turned to chemistry. He loved the class, but his grades didn't reflect his passion. Salk faced long odds applying to medical school: he was a lower middle-class Jew with even lower grades. But Salk stood apart from other applicants because he didn't plan to practice medicine. "I saw myself trying to bring science into medicine."

During his medical school interviews, Salk was warned he wouldn't get rich from research. "There is more to life," he replied, "than money."

> ➡ **What's the role of money in your life? How is that role serving you? How is it serving others?**

If necessity is the mother of invention, curiosity is the father.

Salk's curiosity propelled him forward, and upon his medical school graduation he'd proved that a killed-virus vaccine could provide immunity. On March 1, 1940, Salk became one of twelve interns at Mount Sinai Hospital, likened to "playing ball for the New York Yankees." Two years later, Salk was appointed a research fellow in the University of Michigan's Department of Epidemiology. He received a $2,100 fellowship the same day, a fortunate coincidence since the university position paid nothing.

With mentoring from Thomas Francis, Jr., Salk embarked on research to develop the first influenza vaccine. In autumn of 1945, the U.S. Army vaccinated eight million soldiers, preempting a flu outbreak. As Salk gained notoriety, the relationship between master and apprentice grew strained.

Salk's break came on May 27, 1947, when Max Lauffer invited him to consider leading the University of Pittsburgh's animal virology laboratory. It was a gamble for Lauffer because Salk's reputation was growing and the school was undistinguished and underfunded. To Salk, it offered "the prospect of independence," and he accepted.

The independence Salk perceived was misleading. Despite plenty of red tape and restraints, Salk persevered, expanding his lab staff in anticipation of March of Dimes funding. More importantly, Salk inspired his team with the belief each would play a significant role conquering polio.

By 1951, twenty-eight thousand new cases of polio were recorded. The forecast for 1952 was higher, so Salk decided to inject the vaccine they'd been developing into human patients. On July 2, 1952, forty-three children received the vaccine. Results proved favorable.

On April 26, 1954, more than 1.8 million schoolchildren served as human guinea pigs—unimaginable today, but indicating the fear gripping America. The inoculation became the largest trial in history, financed and operated by volunteers using pencils and paper to track results.

The vaccine was pronounced safe on April 12, 1955. Salk was forty.

➡ **What's the next great thing you and your colleagues will accomplish together?**

Though Salk never sought a patent—"How could you patent the sun?" he asked—his vaccine eradicated one of history's deadliest diseases and is one of the World Health Organization's "Essential Medicines."

Emily Post Begins Work on *Etiquette*

How Civility and Manners Were Made Accessible (and Made to Matter) for Everyone

> "Good manners reflect something from inside—an innate sense of consideration for others and respect for self."
>
> **—EMILY POST**

Acts of kindness reflect a person's character.

Confucius espoused the principle we call the Golden Rule: "Do not do to others what you do not want done to yourself." Christ commanded his followers, "Love your neighbor as yourself," a belief many religions share as the Law of Reciprocity.

Today, dysfunction and disengagement cost companies billions. Have we become so self-centered, so entitled, so discourteous that we no longer place any value on how we treat others?

At high-performing organizations, respect and courtesy are the norms; fun, fulfillment, and profits the byproducts.

Yet for every organization that's a magnet for top talent, there are hundreds more led by people who don't believe respect and courtesy matter or who merely pay lip service to those concepts. Scratching below the surface at these organizations reveals behavior out of sync with the ideals posted on corporate walls and websites.

➡ **If an organization's culture is the sum of its behavior, what would an impartial observer visiting your workplace see, hear, and experience? How do your beliefs compare with how you behave? What's causing this behavior?**

Emily Post was raised in privilege, the daughter of a prominent architect.

Her wedding to New York stockbroker Edwin Main Post ended in scandal when one of Edwin's mistresses blackmailed him. In Emily's 1904 novel *Flight of the Moth*, she wrote of "The eleventh commandment: 'Thou shalt not be found out.'" Appearances mattered to Emily Post. The publicity—more than the infidelity—was humiliating. Emily and Edwin divorced the following year.

With her marriage over, Emily embarked on a career. By 1910, she'd written five novels. Her interior design practice was thriving. A 1915 cross-country drive with her oldest son Ned and cousin Alice Beadleston Post was serialized in *Collier's*.

But May 1920 was the life-changing month for Emily Post. Following Ned's wedding that month, *Vanity Fair* editor Frank Crowninshield asked Emily at a dinner party, "Why don't you compose a book on how to behave?" While claiming little interest, the reality is that nine years earlier Emily had expressed her desire to become an advice columnist.

Alerted by Crowninshield, Funk & Wagnalls publisher Richard Duffy called Emily. "Tell Mr. Duffy," she directed her maid, "that Mrs. Post already has an encyclopedia." When Crowninshield learned of this conversation, he corrected Emily: "Not sell you an encyclopedia, darling. He wants you to write one."

With more prompting, Emily Post agreed to "write a book about etiquette. A sensible book. It'll be a small book. I haven't got much to say, and anyway, the whole subject can be reduced to a few simple rules."

Etiquette, published July 1922, contained 250,000 words requiring 627 pages, overflowing with practical advice: "When you see a woman in silks and sables and diamonds speak to a little errand girl or a footman or a scullery maid as though they were the dirt under her feet, you may be sure of one thing; she hasn't come a very long way from the ground herself."

➡️ **How much rudeness shows up in your organization? What is this behavior costing you?**

Emily Post made culture, civility, and manners accessible for everyone.

Her insights struck the right chords, and her timing was impeccable. World War I, wrote Ned Post, "had acted like a big stirring spoon" in America's melting pot as new ways of thinking, a victorious mindset, and a vibrant economy allowed people "previously submerged" to assume new roles in American business and society. These upwardly mobile people, wrote Ned, "wanted to improve themselves."

Before Emily Post's definitive book, etiquette was served up in one of three styles: a stuffy set of rules; secrets allowing "the socially ambitious to squirm into the ranks of good society"; and depictions of socially inept people doing or saying the wrong thing: "When they spoke of the Fall of Troy, he asked, 'Has there been an accident near Albany?'"

During the reign of Louis XIV from 1643 to 1715, the French Court at Versailles used *étiquettes*, "little cards" or "tickets" to remind courtiers to keep off grass and other similar rules. In one sense, proper etiquette could be a person's ticket into the right circles.

Emily Post believed, however, that "Manners are a sensitive awareness of the feelings of others. If you have that awareness, you have good manners, no matter what fork you use."

Etiquette topped the nonfiction charts, and "What would Emily Post do?" became a frequent refrain throughout America. *Life* magazine recognized Emily Post in 1976 and again in 1990 as one of the most important Americans of the twentieth century. The Emily Post stamp was issued in 1998. The Emily Post Institute, established in 1946, is led by Emily Post's great- and great-great-grandchildren.

Today, lack of civility, courtesy, and good manners are among the reasons employee disengagement and dysfunction are so prevalent in the workplace. But good manners never go out of style.

> ➡ **Do your colleagues not know what's right, or do they not care? What steps can you take?**

You're a leader. Your behavior sets the tone. Think about it. Please.

Allies Invade Normandy in World's Largest Military Battle

How the Free World's Biggest Decision Was Decided

> "Farming looks mighty easy when your plow is a pencil and you're a thousand miles from the corn field."
>
> **—DWIGHT D. EISENHOWER**

That the Allied invasion of Europe was imminent was no secret to the Germans.

The secret was when and where.

Invasion planning began in May 1943, months before Dwight D. "Ike" Eisenhower was named Supreme Commander.

Ike liked to quote an old Army maxim: *Plans are worthless, but planning is everything*, recognizing nothing is "going to happen the way you are planning it."

Yet he emphasized, "This operation is planned as a victory,

and that's the way it's going to be. We're going down there, and we're throwing everything we have into it, and we're going to make it a success."

But on June 5, 1944, the worst weather in twenty years was wreaking havoc on months of planning, the lives of hundreds of thousands of military personnel, the world's destiny, and the nerves of commanders on both sides of the English Channel.

Weeks earlier, Field Marshal Erwin Rommel, commanding more than five hundred thousand German troops in France, wrote his wife, "Here the tension is growing from day to day..."

About the same time, General Dwight Eisenhower, commanding nearly three million Allied troops, wrote to his son, "No other war in history has so definitely lined up the forces of arbitrary oppression and dictatorship against those of human rights and individual liberty."

World War II's outcome hung in the balance.

Now on June 5, 1944, Ike faced the free world's biggest decision.

To go or not to go.

He postponed the Allied invasion the day before due to bad weather. Now he had to decide again. To go or not to go.

Tonight, the decision sending thousands of men to France rested solely on Eisenhower's shoulders. He appeared to be "bowed down with worry...as though each of the four stars on either shoulder weighed a ton."

Despite meticulous planning examining every scenario and expecting events to not go as planned, the world's biggest invasion came down to one thing that could not be planned: the weather.

➡ **How thoroughly do you prepare to remove as much guess-work as possible from your decision-making?**

The weather tormented Eisenhower.

Paratroopers needed moonlight. The army needed calm tides to land its men and inwardly blowing winds to clear smoke from shelling. Everyone wanted long daylight hours, plus another three days of clear weather after D-Day to expedite arrivals of men and supplies.

Just three months of 1944 met these requirements. On May 17, Ike decided only three days in June—the 5th, 6th, and 7th—were suitable, and the previous night, he had called off the invasion scheduled for June 5. He had two days left.

Another postponement risked discovery by the Germans, enabling them to answer "when"—now!—and "where"—Normandy, not the Pas de Calais as Adolf Hitler and others believed.

On June 5, at exactly 9:30 p.m., Eisenhower's chief meteorologist, Group Captain James Martin Stagg, opened the briefing. He and his team had no satellites, no weather radar, no computer modeling to rely on—but they were good and Ike trusted them. They were asked to predict the timing, track, strength, and distance of storms. Stagg announced "some rapid and unexpected developments" that added up to a break in the weather.

Ike polled his commanders. It was still a huge gamble, yet all said, "Go."

Only Ike could make the decision. One general noted "the isolation and loneliness" of Ike as "he sat, hands clasped before him, looking down at the table"; some said two minutes passed, others as many as five.

Then Eisenhower looked up and said slowly, "I am quite positive we must give the order. I don't like it, but there it is."

> ➡ **The four cornerstones of trust are shared values, clarity of purpose, skills mastery, and proven performance. Where in your organization are these cornerstones the shakiest?**

In the early hours of June 6, 1944, Eisenhower watched as the first of 882 planes carrying thirteen thousand men took off for France. Tears filled his eyes.

Meanwhile, German leaders were fighting two wars: one with the Allies, the other with Hitler's erratic decision-making.

Hitler and most German officers believed the Allies would not attack in weather this bad. They were wrong.

Hitler had ordered a military exercise in Rennes, a two-hour drive from Normandy's beaches, so there were no senior officers on the front.

The Luftwaffe had only 183 fighter planes in France, and 124 were transferred from the coast the day before the invasion. And 16,242 seasoned Panzer troops were on alert 25 miles (40 km) southeast of Caen, awaiting Hitler's personal order.

Hitler retired for the night as the first Allied paratroopers were dropping into France. Hitler's aide, Admiral Karl Jesko von Puttkamer, found initial reports "extremely vague" and "feared that if I woke him at this time he might start one of his endless nervous scenes which often led to the wildest decisions."

It was the beginning of the end of Hitler's Third Reich.

➡ How is your behavior as a leader preventing you from getting the best information, the most honest input, and the wisest counsel from those you count on most?

Ike made the tough decision to win the Allies' Great Crusade. What tough decisions must you make to win yours?

The Beatles Audition with George Martin

How a Producer's Intuition Saw Past the Music

> "If I, too, had turned them down, it's very hard to guess what would have happened. Probably they would have broken up and never have been heard from again."
>
> **—GEORGE MARTIN**

Chances to secure a recording contract were evaporating.

The Beatles had talent, judging from the audiences they drew regularly. Of more than five hundred different groups in the 249 square miles (645 km^2) of Merseyside surrounding The Beatles' hometown of Liverpool, the band sat atop *Mersey Beat*'s first popularity poll released on January 4, 1962.

But to take the next step, The Beatles needed a recording contract.

The group's success or failure hung in the balance in the early months of 1962. Decisions made by manager Brian Epstein and producer George Martin catapulted the group to stardom as The Beatles became the world's most influential music band and the bestselling band in history.

As the band's new manager, Epstein had approached virtually every recording company without success. Then a meeting with Decca Records prompted Mike Smith to catch one of The Beatles' acts on December 13, 1961. The band's performance wasn't good enough to secure a contract, but Smith invited the boys to London for a recorded audition.

The audition was scheduled for New Year's Day in 1962. Instead of celebrations on New Year's Eve, The Beatles drove nine hours in the snow from Liverpool to London, arriving tired and anxious.

The fifteen-song selection to showcase the band's versatility backfired, highlighting a lack of consistency. Even with missed notes, uninspired showmanship, and poor drumming, Mike Smith said, "You should record."

But Smith's boss Dick Rowe had the final say. Facing budget cuts, Rowe told Smith to choose between Brian Poole and The Tremeloes—an easier management job because of the band's proximity and a safer choice given the band's regular BBC radio show—and The Beatles—inconsistent, undisciplined, and 178 miles (287 km) away in Liverpool. Smith picked Brian Poole and The Tremeloes.

While Rowe became known as the man who turned down The Beatles, he signed The Rolling Stones eighteen months later on George Harrison's recommendation.

➡ **If you could go back in time five years, what decision would you make differently? What decision are you making today that you may regret five years from now?**

Following Decca's January rejection, Epstein arranged a February meeting with EMI producer George Martin even though Martin's colleague Sid Coleman noted The Beatles "had been rejected by everybody, absolutely everybody in the country."

At the meeting, Epstein played Martin a tape. "You know," said Martin, hedging his bets, "I really can't judge it on what you're playing me here. Bring them down to London and I'll work with them in the studio."

It wasn't a rejection, but it felt like Decca déjà vu.

When no other options materialized that spring, Epstein met with Martin a second time on May 9, and the producer offered the group a recorded audition in exchange for right of first refusal if things went well.

On June 6, 1962, The Beatles arrived at the EMI studios with thirty-two songs they'd been honing. Martin directed his colleague Ron Richards to select two or three songs to record, and he picked two Lennon-McCartney originals and two other songs.

George Martin and engineer Norman Smith critiqued the playback for John, Paul, George, and Pete Best. Everything was problematic, from the material itself to the group's studio presence.

After an hour-long critique, George Martin asked The Beatles if there was anything they didn't like. George Harrison waited a beat and then pounced: "I don't like your tie." After an uncomfortable silence, George Martin noticed a slight smile from George Harrison and then began laughing. The joke broke the tension, opened a lively bit of wordplay, and gave Martin a glimpse of the boys' wit, chemistry, and potential. But Pete Best had not joined in.

During this animated exchange, Martin made two decisions. He would sign The Beatles despite their mediocre performance, and drummer Pete Best would "have to go."

> **There's a time for analysis and a time for intuition. How do you know when to trust one over the other?**

Under the tutelage of Martin, The Beatles replaced Pete Best with Ringo Starr, released six albums in thirty-three months, and toured internationally nearly nonstop as the group performed more than fourteen hundred concerts. The Beatles achieved worldwide acclaim.

So as John, Paul, George, and Ringo approached their tenth year together, they sought something new.

The group's preparation for an August 1966 U.S. tour and the release that same month of *Revolver*, the group's seventh album, brought into sharp focus three significant conflicts. First, The Beatles knew their music could scarcely be heard above fans' screaming; their shows had become events, not concerts. Second, the group's increasing experimentation in the studio with overdubs, backward recordings, sound effects, and additional musicians playing a variety of instruments meant The Beatles' new music could no longer be performed live. Third, John, Paul, George, and Ringo were bored with touring and worn out from their near-continuous time on the road.

The group decided the U.S. tour would be its last.

Having completed their final tour, band members went their separate ways on a three-month holiday. The time to relax and reflect proved historic.

Conceived by Paul on a flight from Nairobi to London in September 1966, *Sgt. Pepper's Lonely Hearts Club Band* gave the band freedom to experiment musically.

"*Sgt. Pepper* was our grandest endeavor," Ringo recalled. "It gave everybody—including me—a lot of leeway to come up with ideas and to try different material... The great thing about the band was that whoever had the best idea—it didn't matter who—that was the one we'd use... Anything could happen."

Recording the entire album spanned 129 days, or seven hundred hours. Total time spent recording the final track on *Sgt. Pepper*—"A Day in The Life"—took thirty-four hours. Their first album—*Please Please Me*—was recorded in ten hours and forty-five minutes.

Sgt. Pepper was an immediate critical and commercial success, spending twenty-seven weeks atop the UK albums chart and fifteen weeks at number one in the United States, and earning four Grammy Awards.

It's considered one of the earliest and best forms of a concept album and has sold more than thirty-two million copies worldwide.

➡ **Where can we break with convention, the status quo, and the predictable and deliver something new?**

You can do great things, too. You just need a little help from your friends.

Charles Darwin's "Pencil Sketches" Reveal First Theories of Natural Selection

How the Famed Naturalist Connected the Dots

> "I have steadily endeavored to keep my mind free, so as to give up any hypothesis, however much beloved (and I cannot resist forming one on every subject), as soon as facts are shown to be opposed to it."
>
> **—CHARLES DARWIN**

By the time twenty-two-year-old Charles Darwin departed Plymouth, England, aboard the *Beagle* on December 27, 1831, he'd made three life-shaping decisions.

First, Darwin decided to leave the University of Edinburgh Medical School for the University of Cambridge to study theology.

Second, Darwin, swept up in the wave of science engulfing British society, collected beetles, learned taxidermy, and devoured current (and occasionally controversial) books on "religious natural theology." He assisted biologist Robert Edmond Grant with research of marine invertebrates, presenting his findings at age nineteen.

Third, Darwin accepted Robert FitzRoy's invitation to join the *Beagle*'s journey around the world as a naturalist, retaining control over his notes and specimens from the voyage.

Though Darwin's father encouraged Charles's path toward Anglican ministry, Charles's father and grandfather—both prominent physicians—were "freethinkers" with philosophical viewpoints formed on the basis of logic, reason, and empirical data rather than authority and tradition. They viewed traditional religious beliefs with skepticism.

Charles's grandfather Erasmus had published *Zoonomia*, his two-volume medical work containing the idea "the strongest and most active animal should propagate the species"—survival of the fittest. Charles's views on evolution, though informed by his grandfather's writings, later concluded that "natural selection" (a term Charles coined) is based on "adaptation" rather than "strength" and "activity."

⇒ **What big decisions early in your life set you on your course? What did you learn from those decisions?**

The *Beagle*'s first stop off Africa's coast established patterns for the remainder of the voyage: FitzRoy surveyed and charted the coasts; Darwin observed, wrote, sketched, and collected flora and fauna specimens.

"During some part of the day," Darwin recalled of his routine, "I wrote in my Journal, and took much pains in describing carefully and vividly all that I had seen; and this was good practice." For Darwin, nothing "compared with the habit of energetic industry and of concentrated attention." This "habit of mind" during the voyage was the "training which has enabled me to do whatever I have done in science."

On September 15, 1835, the *Beagle* reached the Galápagos Islands. It would be Darwin's only visit. During the next five weeks, an idea lodged in Darwin's mind that germinated for years before bursting upon the world, linking Darwin and these islands forever.

The thirteen major and seven minor islands comprising the Galápagos archipelago lie 620 miles (1,000 km) west of Ecuador. Every animal arrived here through the air or ocean millions of years ago.

The idea that each island was home to a different species was pointed out to Darwin by Nicholas Lawson, vice governor of Galápagos. "The different islands to a considerable extent are inhabited by a different set of beings," Darwin wrote. "My attention was first called to this fact by the Vice-Governor, Mr. Lawson, declaring that the tortoises differed from the different islands, and that he could with certainty tell from which island any one was brought. I did not for some time pay sufficient attention to this statement."

That observation, planted in the subconscious of young Darwin, would prove central to his theory of evolution.

⟹ Where in your life would closer observation be helpful? How do you encourage long-term thinking when success frequently is measured in ninety-day increments?

The two-year voyage of the *Beagle* became an expedition of four years, nine months, and five days.

Darwin, seasick for much of the trip, continued working, sending notebooks and specimens to England. His findings were presented in scientific circles, earning him acclaim.

Darwin departed England a dandy. He returned in 1836 a celebrated naturalist.

His edited notebook was published in 1836 (*Journal*), followed in 1839 by *The Voyage of the Beagle*, both bestsellers. He was elected a Fellow of the Royal Society, Britain's foremost scientific club.

Darwin maintained a belief in God throughout the *Beagle* voyage and for some time thereafter, but by 1939, his theory of evolution "was clearly conceived." He hesitated to discuss it, much less publish it. He did not wish to be theologically subversive. He could not afford to be wrong. Darwin was willing to "give up any hypothesis, however much beloved…as soon as facts are shown to be opposed to it." But Darwin had the facts. Science and religion were on a collision course with one another in Victorian Great Britain.

And so in June 1842, "I first allowed myself the satisfaction of writing a very brief abstract of my theory."

In 1844, he enlarged it, believing it to be "a considerable step in science." *On the Origin of Species* was published on November 14, 1859, causing an immediate sensation because of the controversial theories it introduced about evolution and the implications for Creation.

Beyond its historical, scientific, and even religious significance, Darwin's theories of "natural selection" and "survival of the fittest" are manifestos for today's business leaders.

⇒ **What one thing will you begin to change in the next thirty days that isn't delivering the expected results or that customers (or clients) no longer value? What's the impact of not changing?**

The line separating successful organizations from those that habitually underperform or fail altogether can be such a fine one that leaders, as Darwin suggests, may miss seeing it "until the hand of time reveals it."

Yet that line—while fine—is nevertheless distinct. And often unforgiving.

Lakota, Cheyenne, and Arapaho Annihilate Custer and His Men at Little Bighorn

How Arrogance and Ambition Led to the Bloodiest Day on the American Frontier

> "There are not enough Indians in the world to defeat the Seventh Cavalry."
>
> **—GEORGE ARMSTRONG CUSTER**

Winners, we're told, write history.

Yet the history of the American frontier's bloodiest day was written by the losers.

For nearly one hundred years, Custer's Last Stand was characterized as a heroic engagement led by the daring Boy

General of the Civil War whose vastly outnumbered Seventh Cavalry fought valiantly but eventually was overpowered by Native American warriors.

Much of the truth surrounding the events of June 25, 1876, was whitewashed at the time, romanticized in the aftermath, or simply never fully known because most of the surviving eyewitnesses—the Native American combatants—were not interviewed until decades later.

The Lakota, Cheyenne, and Arapaho tribes were not seeking trouble that day. Far from it. They were following the buffalo herds on which they depended for their existence: food, clothing, shelter. The white man's slaughter of the buffalo brought more tribes into greater proximity, and the Plains tribes gathered in Montana that June for their most important religious event of the year: the Sun Dance.

General George Armstrong Custer was ordered to "round up the hostiles." He imagined a successful outcome of this mission might lead to the presidency of the United States. Clearly Custer was daring; but his determination to prove himself combined with impulsive decision-making produced a volatile leader in search of heroics.

The battle that day was more of an annihilation due to bad judgment, incompetence, indifference, and a skilled and brave adversary who outnumbered Custer ten to one.

Though the Battle of Little Bighorn was not a vital military event, it serves as a reminder to modern leaders to collect facts, assess prevailing conditions, and listen to the voices of experience.

> ⇒ **Where are the gaps in your knowledge and experience that may be skewing your perspective?**

Sunday was the day of reckoning.

Aged thirty-six, Custer was a complicated man who battled American Indians ruthlessly yet admitted he would resist if he were one of them. He was a decorated officer who'd been court-martialed twice in six years. He relished a fight; his style of leadership on the battlefield was poorly suited for peacetime.

Custer's adversaries had gathered in the largest Native American encampment in North America: twelve thousand people. One-third were warriors led by Sitting Bull, whose bravery, political prowess, generosity, and inner strength positioned him as a leader of leaders.

It was Sitting Bull's vision during the Sun Dance that he saw many soldiers "as thick as grasshoppers" falling upside down into the Lakota camp, foreshadowing a victory over a large army.

By sunup that Sunday, Custer's scouts reported large numbers of Indians. If the scouts had seen the enemy, the enemy had seen the Seventh Cavalry. The element of surprise was lost. Fearful the Indians would slip away and scatter, Custer made his first mistake: pursuing his quarry against unknown odds.

At noon, Custer halted his regiment between the valleys of the Rosebud and Little Bighorn Rivers and made his second mistake: splitting his troops into three combat groups and a pack train.

Two hours later, the advance reconnaissance party returned, and scout Mitch Bouyer told Custer, "There are more Sioux than all of your soldiers put together have bullets." All scouts agreed. Custer rebuked them and ordered his troops to move out.

The sun blazed as Custer mounted a ridge and saw below what appeared to be a deserted village. "We've caught them napping," he shouted. It was just after 3:00 p.m. when Custer made his third and final mistake.

"After them, boys! Charge!"

> ➡ **What's your process for proceeding with a decision in the face of data that suggests you shouldn't? How might your ego be clouding your decision-making?**

"Today is a good day to die!"

Crazy Horse yelled the Sioux war cry—*Hoka hey! Follow me / Today is a good day to fight / Today is a good day to die*—as warriors engaged Custer's three separate combat groups.

Major Marcus Reno's unit attacked first, losing half of his 112 men before ordering a disorderly retreat. Reno survived and later was cleared by a court of inquiry for his performance, though the stigma of drunkenness and cowardice that day followed him to his grave.

Captain Frederick Benteen commanded 140 men and failed to comply with Custer's order to reinforce him. His hatred of Custer may have been one reason. He survived the day; his reputation did not.

Custer and three hundred men attacked the village, and Custer was shot in the chest crossing the river. Witnesses recall the fighting spirit immediately left Custer's men, who then dragged their commander to the ridge where the battalion was annihilated twenty minutes after Custer had ordered the attack.

"Reno proved incompetent and Benteen showed his indifference," said survivor William Taylor. "Both failed Custer."

➡ If you found yourself in a tough spot, who are the key people you'd call for help? How would they respond?

Will your troops follow you? Should they?

America's Founding Fathers Deflect Differences to Achieve Common Goal

How Key Decisions in the Summer of 1776 Led to America's Independence

> "The second day of July, 1776, will be the most memorable...in the history of America. I am apt to believe that it will be celebrated by succeeding generations as the great anniversary festival."
>
> **—JOHN ADAMS**

The first battles of the American Revolutionary War were fought in Lexington and Concord on April 19, 1775.

The Battle of Yorktown that culminated on October 19, 1781,

with General Charles Cornwallis's surrender to General George Washington prompted the British government to negotiate the war's conclusion.

But it was during the summer of 1776 that the confluence of so many significant events swelled to a historical climax to shape America's destiny.

In May 1776, the fifty-six delegates of the second Continental Congress were split into three factions: loyalists, reformers, and those favoring independence.

Sometimes it's difficult to discern if the decisions you must make will be historic. Other times, you know.

The fifty-six delegates knew they were in the spotlight and they sensed their decisions would be judged by posterity: "We are in the very midst of a revolution, the most complete, unexpected, and remarkable of any in the history of nations," wrote John Adams, one of five Massachusetts delegates and who, nineteen years later, would become America's second president.

And so with British cannon thundering nearby—perhaps heightening the urgency—the delegates found ways of reaching consensus to make monumental decisions over the next three weeks with lightning-quick speed, including approving a proposal for new state constitutions and a 218-word preamble Adams added that was a *de facto* declaration of independence.

They next began debating Richard Henry Lee's resolution "that these United Colonies are, and of right ought to be, free and independent States."

➡ **If you could change your organization, what would it become? What's the first step you can take toward that change?**

Lee's resolution on Friday, June 7, sparked a heated debate that showed no signs of cooling after John Hancock called Congress to order the following Monday. Moderates succeeded in delaying a vote until July 1 to allow the delegates to confer with their state legislatures.

To avoid lost time should the vote for independence pass, Congress appointed the Committee of Five consisting of Adams, Ben Franklin, Thomas Jefferson, Robert Livingston, and Roger Sherman with instructions to prepare a document.

Given his reputation and prowess as a storyteller with *Poor Richard's Almanack*, Franklin, fifty, was the clear favorite to prepare the draft. He declined, saying he wouldn't write anything for review by a committee.

Adams had a sharp legal mind—and tongue. He already chaired twenty-three different committees, including one serving as General George Washington's civilian boss. Adams, forty, also recognized his radical position and hard-charging personality would be a distraction if he authored the document to be discussed.

Next up: Jefferson, who had returned to Philadelphia on May 14 after celebrating his thirty-third birthday in April at Monticello. Jefferson was not the youngest delegate: Thomas Lynch III and Edward Rutledge, each twenty-six, claimed that distinction. Jefferson was painfully shy, a poor public speaker, and an introvert, but his pen did the talking. He also was a Virginian, which was important because of Virginia's economic clout in America and, therefore, its clout in Congress. Jefferson was less controversial than Adams. And, as Adams noted, Jefferson could "write ten times better" than the others.

Jefferson would have preferred to return home to revise Virginia's constitution. Destiny called.

➡ **Where are you getting in the way? What might happen if you invited your best people regardless of age, tenure, or position to help you plan the future?**

In its first meeting on June 11, the Committee of Five agreed on the document's framework, and then turned over the writing to Jefferson.

Working on a laptop desk of his own invention, Jefferson thought, wrote, and rewrote the draft, using elegiac language to frame the argument for independence with potent ideas (he changed the word "subjects" in his draft to "citizens").

Meanwhile, in the days following Adams's May 12 resolution, state legislatures were notifying Congress of their support for independence. Jefferson shared his draft with Franklin and Adams on June 21, and it was here the phrase "We hold these truths to be sacred and undeniable" was changed to "self-evident."

The draft was presented to Congress on Friday, June 28, 1776, as the British fleet carrying nine thousand redcoats anchored off the Long Island coast.

Over the next three days, Congress made eighty-five revisions, focusing on the grievances outlined in the document and all but ignoring Jefferson's inspiring opening.

The signers of the Declaration of Independence deliberately skirted the difficult issues of slavery, women's rights, and civil rights. Adams's intent during the debates was to keep everyone's eyes on the prize: independence. Other issues, Adams argued in what many consider the most significant speech of his distinguished career, would have to wait.

Of the hundreds of decisions made that summer, the crucial decision came on July 2 with a unanimous vote for independence.

Now Washington had to win the war. Careening from one defeat to another, Washington experienced an epiphany: he could achieve America's goal of independence by not losing.

As the summer of 1776 closed, Washington executed a miraculous retreat from New York on August 31. He and his army would live to fight another day.

They would be fighting a war against the world's mightiest military and economic power to win life, liberty, and the pursuit of happiness.

➡ **What must you be willing to say, do, and set aside to achieve your most important goal?**

Let the fireworks begin.

The Berlin Wall Symbolizes a Culture of Fear

How Regulations, Bullets, and Barbed Wire Failed to Curtail Passion

"So...they built the wall to stop people leaving, and now they're tearing it down to stop people leaving. There's logic for you."

—ANONYMOUS

Berlin has long been a tale of two cities.

Berlin was founded as two villages on opposite banks of the river Spree. The village Cölln was settled by Romans and the village Berlin was settled by Slavs, who named their village *brl*, marsh town.

In 1307 the towns merged, and, for the next three hundred years, grew and prospered. Yet a cauldron of intolerance simmered among Catholics and Protestants, boiling over in 1618 as the

Thirty Years' War, Europe's deadliest war. By 1648, Berlin was reduced to 845 houses and Cölln was wiped out. King Frederick William constructed a wall in 1730 to protect Berlin and to tax travelers entering city gates, but the wall offered little protection from Napoleon, who in 1806 defeated the Prussian army.

As the region drifted from peace and prosperity toward bankruptcy, Otto von Bismarck was appointed prime minister in 1861, embarking on building a world capital on the marshland. Berlin under Bismarck's leadership became a military juggernaut and industrial powerhouse, second only to the United States in steel production and excelling in new areas of electrical and chemical manufacturing. When World War I erupted in 1914 and Bismarck pledged his empire, Germany's technological advances contributed to the deaths of sixteen million soldiers and civilians.

In the twenty-one years between two world wars, Berlin rebuilt, currency stabilized, and the arts and sciences thrived. Germany boasted more Nobel Prize winners in the 1920s than any nation.

Two dangerous political leaders emerged. Though their styles and ideologies were different, they each set their sights on asserting territorial claims left unresolved by World War I.

Adolf Hitler's 1923 coup against Germany's Communists failed. But over the next ten years, Hitler constructed ideological walls around a pro-Aryan sentiment, blaming the Treaty of Versailles, Jews, and Communists for Germany's ills.

Walter Ulbricht was Hitler's Communist opponent. In 1924, Ulbricht traveled to Moscow for training as a political revolutionary. He returned to Germany and by 1929 had become the top Soviet official in Berlin.

Ulbricht's devotion to Communism, tireless work, and rise to power under Stalin positioned him as Russia's leader in post-war Germany. As the United States, Great Britain, France, and the former Soviet Union divided Germany into four zones, and Germany's capital—Berlin—into four sectors, Ulbricht spear-headed the Communists' consolidation of power in Germany as Western powers sought to contain it.

Walls can protect. They also can isolate and exclude.

> ➡ Where have walls—visible and invisible—been erected in your organization? What's the impact of the walls, silos, and cliques in your organization?

Within eight weeks following Germany's surrender, the Soviets had tightened their grip on Berlin.

Fear is a powerful motivator, and Josef Stalin ruled by fear. But maintaining a state of fear is costly and, over the long term, ineffective: Fear breeds suspicion, smothers creativity, and requires relentless enforcement. Fear will drive away the people you value the most.

The non-Communists Ulbricht appointed to lead Soviet efforts in post-war Germany were puppets. The real decision-makers were Communists. "It has to look democratic," said Ulbricht, "but we must have everything in our hands."

When the Allies substituted new Deutsche Marks for Reichsmarks in June 1948, the Soviets retaliated. On June 24, 1948, the Berlin Blockade began and with it the Cold War. Despite aggressive Soviet interference, the Allies airlifted tons of supplies for isolated Berliners.

By 1952, East Germans' standard of living had declined compared to 1947. Three-quarters of Berliners listened to American radio and imagined a better life outside the Soviet sector. Between 1947 and 1953, more than 865,000 people left East Germany—a literal brain drain of the brightest minds.

In the mistaken belief that walls curtail thinking, Ulbricht recommended installing barbed wire fencing at Germany's inner borders. Berlin soon would be next.

➡ What are you kidding yourself about?

Stalin's successor Nikita Khrushchev saw America's new young president John F. Kennedy as someone he could intimidate, using Soviet successes with Sputnik as a nuclear threat.

At a June 1961 summit in Vienna between Khrushchev and Kennedy, Berlin symbolized Soviet–American tension. Khrushchev blustered, bullied, and bluffed. Kennedy remained cool, but, despite hours of advance briefing, was unprepared for Khrushchev's fierce determination to expand communism worldwide.

Publicly, Ulbricht said, "No one has the intention of building a wall." Privately, Ulbricht warned his Moscow masters that Berlin was "growing visibly worse." He recommended building a wall. Khrushchev, vacationing in the Crimea the first week in July, decided to build it. Ulbricht tipped off his lie: it was the first use of the word "wall."

Building the Berlin Wall was a monumental undertaking of logistics and secrecy. On August 12, 1961, Russian puppets rubber-stamped Khrushchev's order to close the border and erect a wall. At midnight, more than thirty-six thousand police, army, and militia installed barbed wire entanglements along the 97 miles (156 km) of the three western sectors and the 27-mile (43 km) division of West and East Berlin. Residents awoke on "Barbed Wire Sunday" to find themselves trapped.

In June 1987, President Ronald Reagan challenged Soviet Premier Mikhail Gorbachev, "Mr. Gorbachev, tear down this wall!" On November 9, 1989, the wall fell. Two years later, so did the Soviet Union.

> ➡ **What must happen for you to tear down the walls in your organization and unite your people?**

Boundaries and walls can be helpful. The Berlin Wall failed spectacularly.

John Roberts Becomes Black Bart

How a Good Sailor Became the World's Most Successful Pirate

> "When all the hazard that is run for it, at worst, is only a sour look or two at choking. No, a merry life and a short one, shall be my motto."
>
> **—JOHN ROBERTS**

Every organization has pirates.

Workplace pirates don't wield cutlasses, but they're dangerous. They're the employees who deliver tremendous results but don't play by the rules. They may get the job done, but it's at the expense of those around them. So it's important you know how to handle pirates on board your ship.

The 1650s to 1730s marked the Golden Age of Piracy when pirates like Blackbeard, William Kidd, and Henry Morgan gained fame and fortune for their buccaneering exploits in the Caribbean, the eastern Pacific, the Indian Ocean, and the Red Sea.

But these pirates pale in comparison to the success of pirate John Roberts.

John Roberts's route from honest sailor to the most successful pirate of them all can be traced over a six-week period that began with his capture by pirates off the coast of Africa on June 6, 1719.

Roberts's life started innocently in South Wales in a family of devoutly religious farmers. They didn't have much, so tales of Welsh pirates like John Callis and fantasies of buried treasure fired the imagination of a boy trapped in a village with few prospects for a better life.

Though the life of a sailor involved backbreaking work where the food was sickening, sleep was hard to come by, and the ship's hierarchy could be enforced brutally, it was a life that promised young Roberts escape from his current existence, so at age thirteen he left home and joined a ship's crew.

Two of the hardest questions any of us must answer for ourselves are "Who am I?" and "What do I want?" Roberts didn't yet know who he was, but he knew for certain he wanted a new life.

➡ **What's the biggest thing that's missing in your life? What steps must you take to put yourself on a better path?**

Little is known of Roberts's early sailing years other than he toiled as a third mate on merchant and slaver ships, distinguished himself as a navigator, and, somewhere along the way, changed his named to Bartholomew Roberts.

Roberts was never called Black Bart in his lifetime. It was a name that stuck after fellow Welshman I. D. Hooson's poem described the pirate's "black" complexion.

Nor did the test of Roberts's character occur the day of his capture. Pirates, always in need of officers, had dragged Roberts aboard unwillingly on June 6, 1719.

At the time of his capture, Roberts began to realize that, despite his skills, the navy offered him no path to a captaincy. At thirty-seven, he was running out of time. But being ten years older than most of the crewmen had its advantages, and his stature, intellect, and discipline made Roberts a natural leader.

Repulsed though he was by pirates' undisciplined life, his six weeks of captivity provided a glimpse of a better future for himself, illegal though it was. "In an honest service," Roberts later said, "there is thin commons [resources], low wages, and hard labor; in [piracy, there is] pleasure and ease, liberty and power."

When the captain of Roberts's ship died during a failed raid, the pirates voted for new leadership. Roberts became a pirate that second week in July 1719 when he accepted command of the *Royal James.*

Roberts changed his principles because he was seduced by power.

"I have dipped my hands in muddy water," said Roberts upon his acceptance, "and if a pirate I must be, 'tis better being a commander than a common man."

> ⇒ **What are your guiding principles? What are your non-negotiables—the principles you are unwilling to compromise?**

Having grown up poor, Roberts understood pirates' hatred of anyone prosperous.

Pirates believed the bounty they plundered was their rightful reward for what an honest life had unfairly denied them.

But upon being named captain, Roberts knew more discipline was required.

Say what you will about pirates, they had rules, known as Articles, that governed life aboard a ship and that everyone was required to sign. One of Roberts's first acts was to create a new set of Articles—eleven in all.

Only those dedicated to a life of piracy would choose to sign such a document. Roberts's crew of cut-throats willingly signed their own death warrant.

Yet they also were signing up to follow the most successful pirate who ever sailed the high seas.

By the time he was killed by British sailors three years after becoming a pirate, Roberts had captured about four hundred ships, commanded more men, and sailed 35,000 miles (56,327 km)—far more than any other pirate.

A pirate's success hinged on a monarch's willingness to tolerate him until the pirate had grown so powerful, stolen so much property, and killed so many people that the bad behavior could no longer be tolerated or ignored. At that point, a government would invest the necessary time, money, people and—occasionally—blood to bring a pirate to justice.

> ➡ Who are those in your organization who are producing results at the expense of your core values? What's your plan for addressing this behavior?

With pirates, there will always be a bad ending. Failure to be clear about the behavior you expect means things will end badly for you instead of the pirate.

Edward Whymper and His Team Are the First Climbers to Ascend the Matterhorn

How Success Turned without Warning to Disaster

> "[The Matterhorn] was the last great Alpine peak which remained unscaled—less on account of the difficulty of doing so than from the terror inspired by its invincible appearance."
>
> **—EDWARD WHYMPER**

Mountaintop experiences can be energizing. They also can be deadly.

As you consider your climb toward a lofty objective, remember that there's danger at the top.

Edward Whymper earned a reputation as the greatest

mountaineer of his time. When English publisher William Longman sent him to the Alps in July 1860, it was to sketch them, not to climb them.

Returning from an afternoon of sketching, Whymper decided to return by a different route. His path across the Gorner Glacier became increasingly difficult, and as night fell, Whymper, traveling alone, found himself in a precarious position. Ahead of him lay a sheer, smooth cliff he could not climb without an axe; behind him was a crevasse he first believed he could not jump. Now, there was no alternative but to jump. An unsuccessful jump meant death.

He asked himself, "Can it be done?" His answer: "It *must* be!"

Whymper tossed his walking stick and sketchbook across the crevasse, backed up as far as the mountainside allowed, then ran, leaped, and made it. Stones showered the spot where he had stood minutes before. It was exhilarating.

Whymper was twenty years old.

The following year, Whymper returned to the Alps, urged "by those mysterious impulses which cause men to peer into the unknown." He became the first to summit Mont Pelvoux in Dauphiné, France.

Whymper next turned his sights on the Matterhorn. He was attracted by its "grandeur" and the challenge that it was "considered to be the most completely inaccessible of all mountains."

Standing 14,692 feet (4,478 m) above sea level, the Matterhorn, in Whymper's view, had no rivals in the Alps and but few in the world. Becoming the first to reach the Matterhorn's summit was a race to the top.

⇒ **As you set out to accomplish what few have ever done, what preparations have you shortchanged?**

Whymper first attempted to reach the Matterhorn's summit in August 1861.

Following a bitterly cold night on the mountain, Whymper and his guide awoke to brilliant sunlight illuminating the Matterhorn and providing warmth. Though Whymper could ascend the Matterhorn's "Chimney," his guide could not. Sensing danger if he proceeded alone, Whymper turned back.

Whymper tried again the following July. Approaching the Matterhorn's "Great Staircase," he slipped and fell nearly 200 feet (61 m). Another 10 feet (3 m) would have carried him over the edge to his death 800 feet (244 m) below.

He tried again two weeks later on July 23, but the weather did not cooperate. A fourth try two days later was abandoned.

In total, Whymper made seven unsuccessful attempts to ascend the Matterhorn.

The incentives to be first were as high as the Matterhorn. The commercial value of getting there first was inconsequential and not really considered. The psychological stakes were significant: personal pride, patriotic bragging rights, international recognition. Stakes similar to those in the race to the moon one hundred years later.

Whymper refused to accept defeat. With each unsuccessful attempt, Whymper found himself "longing, more than before, to make the ascent, and determined to return, if possible with a companion, to lay siege to the mountain until one or the other was vanquished."

⇒ **Do you have the mental toughness, financial wherewithal, and executional urgency to see your dream become reality? What's your evidence?**

By July 1865, it appeared likely that one of two teams would be the first to reach the Matterhorn's peak.

Whymper's British party consisted of four guides and three other mountaineers beside himself: Lord Francis Douglas, the Reverend Charles Hudson, and Douglas Hadow, an inexperienced climber.

An Italian team of Quintino Sella and Felice Giordano was led by guide Jean-Antoine Carrel. The Italians started several days earlier but were delayed by weather.

On July 13, 1865, Whymper's party began their ascent, taking a new route on the east face of the mountain Whymper suggested. By noon, the party reached 11,000 feet (3,353 m) and decided to camp and finish the climb to the top the following morning.

When dawn broke the next day, Whymper's party began climbing. After several hours, they discovered 200 feet (61 m) of easy snow between themselves and the summit. "At 1:40 p.m. the world was at our feet," Whymper exclaimed, "and the Matterhorn was conquered."

Whymper's party peered below and saw the Italian team several hundred feet beneath them. Whymper's team had won the race.

The victorious team stayed on the Matterhorn's summit for "one crowded hour of glorious life."

Triumph turned quickly to tragedy. Within the first hour of descent, the inexperienced climber lost his footing and pulled three of his climbers over the edge to their death. The bodies of French guide Michel Croz and Englishmen Charles Hudson and Douglas Hadow were recovered; nothing of Lord Francis Douglas was found but gloves, a boot, a belt, and his watch, stopped at 3:45.

"Climb if you will," said Whymper, "but remember that courage and strength are naught without prudence, and that a momentary negligence may destroy the happiness of a lifetime."

> ⇨ Achieving your objective requires pragmatism and commitment. Commitment always carries a cost. Will the victory be worth it?

Three days after Whymper's ascent, four men reached the summit. The Matterhorn was the last great Alpine peak to be climbed, and its first ascent marked the end of the Golden Age of Alpinism.

Vince Lombardi Holds First Practice with the Green Bay Packers

How a Team of Losers Became Perennial Champions

> "Winning is a habit. Unfortunately, so is losing."
>
> **—VINCE LOMBARDI**

If you're a leader, you're a coach.

Every team—in sports, business, government, academia, not-for-profit—has a roster of talented people. Some leaders are better than others at bringing out the best in their people.

In 1957, the Green Bay Packers finished Coach Lisle Blackbourn's fourth straight losing year with a 3–9 record. He was replaced for the 1958 season by Ray "Scooter" McLean, whose team posted a 1-10-1 record for a last-place finish in the National Football League and the Packers' worst record in their thirty-nine-year history.

The club had hit rock bottom.

The locker room split with the offense and defense pointing fingers at each other. The players liked McLean, "but he had no leadership qualities," remembers the Packers' Gary Knafelc. "If you've been around ballplayers, you know they'll take you to the hilt every time…And we took Scooter in every way."

The Packer franchise was unique because one thousand citizens bought shares in the club in 1950, raising $125,000 and preventing the team from moving to a bigger city. The shareholders elected a forty-five-person committee, which selected a thirteen-person executive committee that ran the team. Or tried to. The team had lost seventy-two games in the 1950s while winning only half that many. The shareholders demanded improvement. Talk swirled about replacing the executive committee. The other NFL owners wanted Commissioner Bert Bell to eject the Packers from the league.

A new coach was needed. Who would risk making that decision? What coach would take a job in the NFL's "salt mines of Siberia"?

> ➡ **How bad must things get before you decide to change?**

The executive committee began its search following the January 1959 draft.

Rumors abounded. One name continued to surface. Vince Lombardi.

Aged forty-five and with no head coaching experience, Lombardi, many believed, was too old for the job. Yet Lombardi was the fiery offensive mastermind of the champion New York Giants.

After being turned down by one coach and passing on the popular "Curly" Lambeau, the executive committee presented Lombardi on January 28 as its choice as the next Packers coach. The know-it-all shareholders were incredulous. *Curly made this town—how can we turn away from him now? Why should we put so much trust in a guy from New York who's never run anything in his life?*

But the executive team had the votes; twenty-six members voted "yes" for Lombardi, one voted "no," and eighteen abstained.

When Lombardi traveled to Green Bay in February to sign his contract, he met the board at a luncheon and outlined his football philosophy: *a power offense built around the running game; a 4–3 defense; players who are in shape and will listen to what I say—if they don't they'll be gone.*

"I want it understood," Lombardi then told the shareholders, "I'm in complete command here. I expect full cooperation from you. You will get full cooperation from me in return. I've never been associated with a loser and I don't expect to be now."

⮕ **Who's running your business? You or someone (or something) else?**

Before Lombardi arrived, one sportswriter compared the Packers' offense to "a conga dance: 1, 2, 3, and kick."

Arriving after the December and January drafts, Lombardi nevertheless built a formidable team.

True to his word, Lombardi sent prima donnas packing, including trading the Packers' best receiver to the Cleveland Browns for three players who would become defensive stalwarts.

Incredibly, the underachieving 1958 team was loaded with

future Hall of Famers, including Bart Starr, Forrest Gregg, Paul Hornung, Ray Nitschke, Jim Ringo, and Jim Taylor, as well as future All-Pros Jerry Kramer, Ron Kramer, Max McGee, Bill Forester, and Dan Currie.

But sixteen veterans from the previous season were sent packing.

On July 23, 1959, at a dinner attended by fifty-six players before the first day of training camp, Lombardi set the tone: "Gentlemen, we're going to have a football team here, and we're going to win some games. Do you know why? You are going to have confidence in me and my system. By being alert, you are going to make fewer mistakes than your opponents. By working harder, you are going to out-execute, out-block, and out-tackle every team that comes your way. I've never been a losing coach and don't intend to start here. There is no one big enough to think [he]…can do what he wants. Trains and planes are coming in and leaving Green Bay every day, and he'll be on one of them. I won't. I'm going to find thirty-six men who have the pride to make any sacrifice to win. There are such men. If they're not here, I will get them. If you're not one…you might as well leave right now."

If Lombardi was in your face, it meant he saw your potential.

> → **Who on your team is waiting for you to help them bring out their best?**

"Perfection is not attainable," Lombardi believed, "but if we chase perfection we can catch excellence." The 1959 Packers finished 7–5 and Lombardi was named Coach of the Year.

Lombardi led the team to five NFL Championships in seven years and won the first two Super Bowls following the 1966 and 1967 NFL seasons.

Today, the Super Bowl is viewed by millions of people worldwide, and the winner of that game is awarded the Lombardi Trophy.

Andrew Hamilton Presents Novel Defense in John Peter Zenger Libel Trial

How Freedom of the Press Was Born

> "The laws of our country have given us a right—the liberty—of exposing and opposing arbitrary power...by speaking the truth."
>
> **—ANDREW HAMILTON**

John Peter Zenger was in jail, awaiting trial for the crime of telling the truth.

Zenger was an unlikely defendant. Emigrating from Germany with his family when he was thirteen, Zenger served an eight-year apprenticeship to William Bradford, New York's first printer. Following a brief partnership together, Zenger established his own printing firm in Manhattan in 1730.

Though Zenger published America's first arithmetic text-book, his business struggled. Not until New York's royal governor died in 1731 and William Cosby was named his replacement did Zenger's business improve and, in the process, cement Zenger's place in history.

Cosby had been forced to repay £10,000 for misappropriating supplies in his previous post. Arriving in New York in August 1732, Cosby sought to rebuild his wealth, demanding half the acting governor's salary though he'd done nothing to earn it. Cosby removed judges he couldn't control and abused laws he'd sworn to uphold, quickly earning a reputation as an obnoxious, oppressive, and greedy bureaucrat.

An anti-Cosby faction formed that included James Alexander, New York's most successful attorney.

In early eighteenth-century England, "seditious libel" meant anything printed that challenged authority and portrayed officials unflatteringly. British law prohibited such reports because they undermined authority.

Truth, therefore, was not considered a defense. The guilty were imprisoned (sometimes for life) or executed.

As Cosby's abuses continued, pamphlets attacking him—many written by Alexander using aliases and printed by Zenger—appeared. When Cosby bent rules in an October 1733 election, the anti-Cosby faction decided to start a newspaper to counter the pro-Cosby *New York Weekly Gazette*. One week after Lewis Morris defeated Cosby's candidate, James Alexander offered Zenger funds—and legal defense, if necessary—to print it.

While Zenger's business needed the money, he accepted the risks to help topple a governor he loathed.

➡ **What ideas are you fighting for?**

On Monday, November 5, 1733, the first edition of the four-page *New York Weekly Journal* rolled off Zenger's press.

The *Journal's* purpose, said Alexander, was "Chiefly to expose [Cosby] and those ridiculous flatteries," noting that Cosby has "given more distaste to the people than I believe any [other] governor."

While the *Journal's* articles never attacked Cosby by name, their target was clear. The articles' authors—chiefly Alexander and Lewis Morris, both lawyers—dodged libel charges through careful phrasing while hiding behind pen names. Editors could not hide: Zenger's name appeared on every edition.

In January 1734, Cosby directed Chief Justice James DeLancey to seek Zenger's indictment for seditious libel. The grand jury refused. Cosby then directed the legislature to order offensive editions burned. The Assembly refused. Cosby appealed to the Governor's Council, inviting to this meeting only those who would do his bidding. True to form, the Council ordered Zenger's arrest.

Six days later, Lewis Morris sailed for England to seek Cosby's removal.

For a third time, the grand jury refused to indict Zenger. But on January 28, 1735, Attorney General Richard Bradley charged Zenger by "information"—a process allowing the government discretion in bringing a person to trial—for printing "false, scandalous, malicious, and seditious" reports. Zenger remained imprisoned, awaiting trial.

Alexander continued behind-the-scenes writing, the *Journal* continued publication, and New Yorkers couldn't get enough. Second press runs of the newspaper met increasing demand.

Attorneys James Alexander and William Smith approached Zenger's case on political rather than legal merits, arguing to Chief Justice DeLancey he should recuse himself because of his improper appointment by Cosby. In response, DeLancey disbarred Alexander and Smith.

New York's two best lawyers were now unable to defend Zenger.

➡ **In what areas are you struggling? Who will you turn to for help?**

DeLancey appointed as Zenger's attorney John Chambers, an inexperienced lawyer loyal to Cosby.

Alexander invited Andrew Hamilton to represent Zenger. Hamilton, fifty-nine, was speaker of the Pennsylvania Assembly, second in power to the governor. He was a brilliant lawyer with "confidence which no terror could awe" and deft courtroom skills unmatched in the colonies.

On August 4, 1735, Chambers concluded his opening remarks on behalf of Zenger. Alexander had kept secret Hamilton's role, so when the Philadelphia lawyer rose to address the court, the air was electric.

Hamilton admitted Zenger had printed and published the newspapers. Hamilton argued, "the words themselves must be libelous—that is, false, scandalous, and seditious—or else we are not guilty."

DeLancey would not allow the words as evidence. Hamilton

replied that he'd never "met with an authority that says we cannot be admitted to give the truth in evidence."

With that door closed, Hamilton risked DeLancey's wrath and Zenger's case by turning his back on the judge and presenting the case directly to the jurors. The judge and prosecuting attorney were no match for Hamilton. This case, Hamilton said, "is not the cause of one poor printer…it is the cause of liberty."

Hamilton encouraged the jurors to disregard the judge's instructions. "As the verdict (whatever it is) will be yours," counseled Hamilton, "you ought to refer no part of your duty to the discretion of other persons."

The jury deliberated ten minutes before returning a verdict of not guilty.

⟶ **What's it like to speak truth to power in your organization?**

While Zenger's acquittal did not change the law of libel, the landmark case inspired Patriots during the American Revolution, informed the Bill of Rights, and laid the foundation for freedom of the press.

Steve Jobs Rescues Apple from Insolvency

How the "Think Different" Campaign Exemplified the Risky Idea to Celebrate Lifestyle, not Technology

> "We have to prove that Apple is still alive and that it still stands for something special."
>
> **—STEVE JOBS**

The summer of 1997 was a desperate time for Apple.

Since Gil Amelio's arrival eighteen months earlier to replace Steve Jobs, things had gone from bad to worse. The company had lost $1.7 billion and still there was no strategy to reverse Apple's plummeting sales.

Seeking a spark, Amelio invited Jobs to return to Apple following the purchase of NeXT. In a meeting called by Amelio and attended by Jobs, advertising agency BBDO presented a new ad campaign proclaiming "We're back."

Everyone expressed their approval except Jobs, who said

that "the slogan was stupid because Apple wasn't back." Feeling "insulted," BBDO quit.

Jobs's assessment was accurate. When board members met in June, Apple's market share was 2.6 percent and falling. The advertising wasn't working. Enormous financial losses were crippling the company. And with no breakthrough products on the horizon, Apple's stock was at a three-year low.

By July 8, Amelio was dismissed. The board initiated a search for a CEO and asked Jobs, forty-two, to fix product development and marketing.

If you stepped into a situation where virtually everything was either broken or not working, where would you start?

Steve Jobs's first step was to simplify. Amelio cut costs. Jobs did too, but he did it differently.

In less than three weeks, Jobs examined every project at Apple, asking project leaders one by one to defend their existence.

But what's a gem and what's garbage? It's true that a smart way to know what your customers want is to ask them, and this practice is often overlooked. But there's more to developing the next big thing than that.

"Our job is to figure out what they're going to want before they do," said Jobs. "I think Henry Ford once said, 'If I'd asked customers what they wanted, they would have told me, "A faster horse!"' People don't know what they want until you show it to them. That's why I never rely on market research. Our task is to read things that are not yet on the page."

To do this, Jobs simplified. But simplifying carried big risks. One of his first major decisions that summer was cutting 70 percent of Apple's product line to "get back to the basics."

> What's your organization's focus? Where can you simplify? What must you eliminate?

In early July, Jobs called Lee Clow of TBWA\Chiat\Day, the mastermind behind Apple's iconic "1984" commercial. Jobs invited Clow to Cupertino, California, to discuss Apple's advertising.

At the meeting, Jobs told Clow and colleague Rob Siltanen that he was inviting other agencies to pitch for the business. Clow and Siltanen were surprised because they figured their past performance would prompt Jobs to award TWBA\Chiat\Day Apple's business without a review.

Surprise number two was Jobs's approach. "I'm thinking no TV ads," said Jobs, "just some print ads in the computer magazines until we get things figured out," to which Siltanen countered, "Half the world thinks Apple is going to die. A few print ads in the computer magazines aren't going to do anything for you. You need to…do something bigger and bolder."

"Fine," snapped Job, "show me the ideas and executions that you guys think are best."

Back in Los Angeles, the agency team discussed how to stand out and strike a chord for Apple that would be relevant and, ultimately, inspiring. They had less than three weeks. They began by asking and answering a few simple questions about Apple.

> Who are we? What do we stand for? Where do we fit?

Given the timeline, the agency dispensed with developing a creative brief and instead gathered market intel about Apple's strengths and weaknesses. Within days, photos, pencil sketches, rough layouts, and possible taglines filled the agency's conference room walls.

One idea stood out: a billboard campaign featuring black-and-white photos of groundbreaking people with Apple's logo and the words "Think Different." It was the work of Craig Tanimoto.

"IBM," Tanimoto explained, "has a campaign out that says 'Think IBM' [it was a campaign for their ThinkPad], and I feel Apple is very different from IBM, so I felt 'Think Different' was interesting. I then thought it would be cool to attach those words to some of the world's most different-thinking people."

On Sunday, August 3, 1997, a small group from TWBA\Chiat\Day flew to Cupertino, and Clow presented the idea to Jobs. "Here's to the crazy ones," the new Apple commercial began. Decisions made that August repositioned Apple from a technology company to a premium lifestyle brand. The rest is history.

When Jobs presented a rough cut of the commercial to a core group of Apple leaders, he framed it this way: "This is a very complicated world; it's a very noisy world. And we're not going to get a chance to get people to remember much about us. No company is. So we have to be really clear on what we want them to know about us."

When the ad debuted on September 27, 1997, Rob Siltanen noted the campaign caused people who "once thought of Apple as semi-cool but semi-stupid to suddenly think about the brand in a whole new way."

➡ **Where are we falling behind? What will you do about it?**

A few weeks earlier, Apple was nearly insolvent. "Think Different" resonated with people and helped make Apple one of the most valuable companies on the planet.

Every leader has the opportunity to change the world. Are you crazy enough to try?

Doane Robinson Persuades Gutzon Borglum to Travel to the Black Hills

How Mother Nature, Vision, and Hard Work Created the World's Biggest Sculpture

> "Every successful enterprise requires three men—a dreamer, a businessman, and a son-of-a-bitch."
>
> **—PETER McARTHUR**

Mount Rushmore is the world's biggest sculpture.

Eight hundred tons of stone were removed from this South Dakota mountain as the faces of George Washington, Thomas Jefferson, Abraham Lincoln, and Theodore Roosevelt were carved, each face taller than Egypt's Great Sphinx.

The Rushmore memorial covers 1,278.45 acres (2 square mi; 5.17 km²) and is 5,725 feet (1,745 m) above sea level. Before the

Alps and Himalayas pushed through the earth's crust, the Black Hills presided over America's northern Great Plains, gray granite exclamation points framed by the Mississippi River on the east and the Rocky Mountains on the west.

Six hundred thousand centuries after the Black Hills formed, historian Doane Robinson, sixty-seven, thought carving the likenesses of famous people would lure tourists to this still-new state. Robinson was a dreamer. "Tourists," Robinson believed, "soon get fed up on scenery unless it has something of special interest connected with it to make it impressive."

After two sculptors turned him down, Robinson's August 20, 1924, letter to Gutzon Borglum describing "opportunities for heroic sculpture" struck pay dirt. Borglum, fifty-seven, was Robinson's third choice, and, at times, an SOB, but without Borglum's creative genius and refusal to let significant obstacles defeat him, Mount Rushmore would not exist.

The following month, Robinson and Borglum met. Robinson proposed carving the likenesses of Native American Red Cloud, Lewis and Clark, and Buffalo Bill Cody. Borglum persuaded Robinson that American presidents offered a more lasting appeal, saying, "If we pitch the note high enough, we will arouse the nation." That September morning, Robinson and Borglum's visions aligned, agreeing to honor America's two greatest heroes—Washington and Lincoln—and creating a monument to American presidents.

South Dakota senator Peter Norbeck supported their vision, and his friendship with President Calvin Coolidge brought the project enormous political and fund-raising power.

Robinson's visionary salesmanship, Borglum's talent bringing dreams to life, and Norbeck's federal fund-raising prowess was Mount Rushmore's three-legged stool that exists inside every organization: sales, operations, finance.

> ➡ **Do you have the horsepower to achieve your objectives? Of the three key roles in your firm—sales, operations, and finance—where are you strongest? Weakest? Who must you add or develop to complete your team?**

One year later, no money had been raised and no carving had begun. Some viewed Robinson's project as being wasteful spending and a "desecration [of] finished products from God's workshop."

Undeterred, Borglum made his second trip to South Dakota.

Robinson's idea was to situate the monument in the Needles, but Borglum rejected it because the eroded Needles were too thin to support sculpting. On August 11, 1925, Borglum, Robinson, and three others beheld Mount Rushmore's majesty, and Borglum knew he'd found his mountain, declaring, "American history shall march along that skyline."

Reaching Rushmore's summit and admiring its grandeur and southeast exposure to the sun, Borglum experienced an epiphany: "It came over me in an almost terrifying manner that I never had sensed what I was planning. Plans must change. The vastness I saw here demanded it."

But Borglum's plans were in his head. Rushmore was still a dream. Lacking government support, money, and organization (there was no contract with Borglum), Norbeck demanded "a definite plan." While Norbeck recognized Borglum was angering many South Dakotans, Norbeck realized, "We need him more than he needs us."

Norbeck got his plan, Borglum got his contract, and on August 10, 1927, Robinson's vision moved from dream to reality when President Calvin Coolidge dedicated Rushmore.

Eight weeks later, Borglum's team began carving Washington's 60-foot (18.29 m) face. Workers suspended in mid-air, wielding 100-pound jackhammers, battled gravity, exhaustion, weather, and an unpredictable mountain surface. The Great Depression threatened the project: in November 1931, the commission had $500 in assets, $16,000 in debt, and no prospects for funding. In 1932, Norbeck secured federal funding and persuaded President Franklin D. Roosevelt to place Rushmore under the jurisdiction of the National Park Service.

Washington's likeness was dedicated on Independence Day in 1934.

Thomas Jefferson's image was planned to appear to Washington's right, but after completing half the work, the rock was determined to be unsuitable, so Jefferson's face was dynamited. What seemed to be a setback became an artistic breakthrough: Washington's isolated profile now projects more powerfully, and the afternoon sun highlights the features of Jefferson and Lincoln.

⮕ **What major initiative appears endangered? What can you do to turn a setback into a breakthrough?**

Every person associated with Mount Rushmore gave an extra measure of themselves to realize a dream none could accomplish alone.

And because of the leaders' immense respect for one another, they frequently spoke hard truths to adapt plans, cede control, and keep the project moving.

Robinson was wrong about the monument's subjects and location. Borglum was mistaken about the money and time required (it took three times as much of both). And Norbeck died from cancer before Mount Rushmore was completed.

Working through three American presidencies and battling naysayers, egos, politics, financial hurdles, and Mother Nature over a sixteen-year period, the Mount Rushmore team built America's shrine to democracy.

➡ **When you review your career, what crowning achievement will you celebrate? What legacy will you leave?**

On October 31, 1941—five weeks before Pearl Harbor— Mount Rushmore opened. Today, Mount Rushmore attracts more than three million visitors annually.

Martin Luther King Jr. Delivers "I Have a Dream" Speech

How Setting Aside Prepared Remarks Released a Message from the Heart

> "Darkness cannot drive out darkness; only light can do that. Hate cannot drive out hate; only love can do that."
>
> **—DR. MARTIN LUTHER KING JR.**

"I have a dream."

Dr. Martin Luther King Jr.'s proclamation at the March on Washington for Jobs and Freedom was a catalyst for confronting and changing America's racial prejudice. But on that day, those words were very nearly not spoken.

Civil rights leaders fretted about the event from its inception until they awoke on August 28, 1963, to see two hundred fifty thousand people peacefully gathered.

Before this day, protests were smaller, and meaningful results were negligible. This march required a bold vision, sorting hundreds of logistics, raising lots of cash, and putting aside individual agendas. Time was short; federal lawmakers weren't helpful.

King unquestionably would be the headliner, but the idea came from A. Philip Randolph, who in 1925 organized and led the first predominantly African American labor union.

Randolph spent years advocating for better pay and working conditions for porters tending to train passengers. Porters were forced to pay for their food, lodging, and uniforms (sometimes half their wages) and barred from becoming conductors though they performed some of those duties.

As America recovered from the Great Depression through President Franklin D. Roosevelt's New Deal programs, African Americans were less likely to benefit. Despite prewar labor shortages, discrimination against African Americans continued. Roosevelt did little to help. So in 1941, Randolph planned a march on the nation's capital to highlight these inequalities. Under this threat, Roosevelt established the Committee on Fair Employment Practices, allowing African Americans the opportunity for better-paying jobs. The march was canceled.

Now, twenty-two years later, Randolph believed the time was right for a march on Washington.

⇒ **What great idea didn't work out? What would happen if you revived it?**

Desegregation was coming to America—but at a stubbornly slow pace.

The Supreme Court's 1954 unanimous decision in *Brown v.*

Board of Education declared unconstitutional state laws separating black and white students.

On December 1, 1955, Rosa Parks refused to relinquish her seat on a Montgomery, Alabama, bus to a white passenger. Though not the first resister, Parks was viewed by reformers as the best candidate to pursue changes through the legal system. Her case was never tried, but Parks and the resulting bus boycott spearheaded by King became important symbols of the movement.

In Greensboro, North Carolina, Ezell Blair Jr., Franklin McCain, Joseph McNeil, and David Richmond were inspired by King's nonviolent protests emulating Mahatma Gandhi's 1930s practices in India. On February 1, 1960, the four freshmen asked to be served coffee at a Woolworth counter, and when, predictably, were refused service, they remained seated until the store closed that night. The next day, more than twenty black students joined the sit-in. On the third day, more than sixty people participated. On the fourth day, more than three hundred people participated. Sit-ins were replicated across North Carolina before spreading to other Southern states.

On April 3, 1963, civil rights leaders brought the movement to segregation's epicenter: Birmingham, Alabama. Judge W. A. Jenkins issued an injunction against "parading, demonstrating, boycotting, trespassing, and picketing." The reformers announced they would march. On April 12, 1963, King was arrested roughly along with other marchers in front of thousands of African Americans dressed for Good Friday.

America's ugly side was broadcast nightly into the nation's living rooms.

➡ **What belief requires your extraordinary effort to conquer obstacles and achieve unprecedented progress? How much sacrifice are you willing to endure?**

Every step forward by reformers to improve civil rights was countered by others working to reverse the gains. But America's civil rights movement was gathering momentum.

Using paper smuggled in by lawyer Clarence Jones, King on April 16 responded from his ten-by-ten-foot cell to an ad in *The Birmingham Post-Herald* signed by eight white clergymen objecting to "demonstrations...directed and led in part by outsiders."

"Letter from Birmingham Jail" begins with King writing, "I was invited...because injustice is here," noting, "Injustice anywhere is a threat to justice everywhere." He warned that continued resistance to reform "will lead inevitably to a frightening racial nightmare."

King was freed on April 19, and on June 11, the March on Washington was announced. It would commemorate the one hundredth anniversary of the Emancipation Proclamation and culminate on the Lincoln Memorial's steps.

Jones organized King's thoughts into a draft the night before, fully recognizing that "Martin would have to breathe life into them."

King was the next to last speaker and, by all accounts, the crowd grew listless as Washington's notorious humidity took its toll. There also was an air of expectation. *What would Dr. King say?*

King's advisers recommended against referring to "dreams" because "It's trite, it's cliché. You've used it too many times already." But eleven minutes into his sixteen-minute speech, King paused for dramatic effect. Gospel singer Mahalia Jackson shouted, "Tell 'em about the dream, Martin!" To his aides' chagrin, Martin Luther King Jr. set aside his prepared text and spoke from his heart.

➡ **Preparation is vital. How will your personal conviction shine through?**

"There comes a time when one must take a position that is neither safe, nor politic, nor popular, but he must do it because conscience tells him it is right," King once said.

King's vision of racial harmony is historic.

The following year, President Lyndon Johnson signed the Civil Rights Act and King, thirty-five, became the youngest man to win the Nobel Peace Prize.

Branch Rickey Signs Jackie Robinson to Shatter Baseball's Color Barrier

How the Brooklyn Dodgers Defied a "Gentlemen's Agreement" and Beat Racism

> "A box score tells you who made hits and who scored runs. It does not tell you anything about a man's religion nor does it even suggest the color of his skin."
>
> **—BRANCH RICKEY**

If current talent is the best predictor of future performance, it follows you'd want the best people you can get on your team.

You'd commit to providing continuous learning and development opportunities to help your teammates reach their full potential.

In baseball's world, this approach to talent development is

called the "farm system," a process honed to perfection by Branch Rickey, a former professional football and baseball player who became a coach, lawyer, baseball manager, front office executive, and the person who shattered baseball's color barrier.

His gutsy decision to sign Jackie Robinson was decades away when Rickey entered baseball.

Branch Wesley Rickey, raised in Ohio's Scioto County by devout Methodists, was named with Isaiah 11:1 in mind and for John Wesley, Methodism's founder. Rickey grew up appreciating right from wrong, and, athletically inclined, played professional football and baseball after college.

An injured throwing arm cut short his playing career, but his coaching acumen and talent insights overshadowed his on-field performance. Rickey entered the University of Michigan's law school in 1910 and was promptly hired to coach Michigan's baseball team. It is a mark of Rickey's passion and competitiveness that he convinced law school dean Harry Hutchins he could handle law school's heavy workload while coaching the team.

Three seasons later, Rickey joined baseball's St. Louis Browns, managing the team's business operations, including its budding farm system. When the team sold in December 1915, Rickey's contract guaranteed employment, but because he and new owner Phil Ball clashed, Rickey moved to the St. Louis Cardinals in 1917 as president and manager.

World War I interrupted Rickey's baseball career, and in the war's final weeks, Major Rickey commanded more than 150 chemical warfare missions in France.

Returning to the Cardinals in early 1919 reunited him with scout Charley Barrett. Rickey was fired as the Cardinals' manager in 1925 after six mediocre seasons, but his revolutionary approach to talent earned Rickey the opportunity to continue in the front office.

The Cardinals—featuring players scouted, acquired, and developed through Rickey's system—won the World Series in 1926. In his final season with the Cardinals, the club won the 1942 World Series. During Rickey's tenure, the club reached the World Series six times, winning three championships.

➡ **What's your most effective approach to attracting, training, engaging, and retaining people? What's your plan for developing talent?**

Upon joining the Brooklyn Dodgers—named for residents' dexterity in dodging city streetcars—Rickey sized up the roster and advised George V. McLaughlin, the banker who'd saved the Dodgers from bankruptcy, that to field a competitive team, "We are going to have to beat the bushes, and we will take whatever comes out, and that might include a Negro player or two."

"If you are doing this to improve the ball club, go ahead," said McLaughlin. "But if you're doing it for the emancipation of the Negro, then forget it." The Dodgers board approved Rickey's plans in early 1943.

A "gentlemen's agreement" barred black players from the white-owned major and minor professional leagues. "The baseballs were all white," Dodgers pitcher Carl Erskine noted, "and so were all the players."

When Chicago Black Sox players conspired to lose the 1919 World Series, baseball Commissioner Kenesaw Mountain Landis restored public confidence by banning those players for life. But Landis refused to integrate baseball, and his November 25, 1944, death cracked open the door for Rickey.

Integration's door opened wider when Governor Thomas Dewey signed the Fair Employment Practices bill on March 12, 1945, making New York the first state prohibiting discrimination against job applicants and employees on the basis of race, religion, or creed.

Rickey knew the other owners were against him, and picking the wrong player would be catastrophic—for him, his team, his sport, and his country. Rickey had scouted black and Cuban players. He had a thorough understanding of their athletic and personal character. He would need to take one more step before making his monumental decision, and Rickey began the five-minute walk from the Dodgers offices to Plymouth Church.

Reverend Dr. L. Wendell Fifield invited Rickey into his study, but Rickey confessed, "I can't talk with you. I just want to be here." For forty-five minutes, Rickey paced, paused, and paced some more before crying, "I've got it! Wendell, I've decided to sign Jackie Robinson!"

A few days after the *Enola Gay* dropped the atomic bomb over Hiroshima, Rickey summoned scout Clyde Sukeforth to his office and dropped his own bomb: Sukeforth would travel to Chicago where Robinson was playing and invite Robinson to meet with Rickey in Brooklyn.

At 10:00 a.m. on August 28, 1945, Jackie Robinson and Clyde Sukeforth met Rickey in his office. Rickey offered Robinson the opportunity to join the Dodgers organization. "I know you're a good ballplayer," said Rickey. "What I don't know is whether you have the guts." Robinson assured Rickey he did.

➡ **If you were starting over, who would you choose for your team?**

Success isn't always colorblind.

Rickey was excoriated by his fellow owners and received hundreds of death threats from fans. Robinson was the object of horrific racial slurs.

Robinson played one season for Brooklyn's minor league team in Montreal before making his Major League Baseball debut on April 15, 1947.

He won the first Major League Baseball Rookie of the Year Award in 1947, was an All-Star for six consecutive seasons from 1949 through 1954, and won the National League Most Valuable Player Award in 1949—the first black player so honored. Robinson played in six World Series, helping the Dodgers win the 1955 World Series championship.

➡ **What time-honored practices will you challenge to produce better results?**

In 1997, Robinson's uniform number, 42, was retired across all major league teams, the first professional athlete so honored. Every April 15, every player on every professional baseball team wears 42 in tribute to Jackie Robinson.

Frank Capra Buys the Rights to *It's a Wonderful Life*

How Belief in an Idea Celebrated a Leader's Far-Reaching (and Often Overlooked) Impact on Lives

> "I made mistakes in drama. I thought drama was when actors cried. But drama is when the audience cries."
>
> **—FRANK CAPRA**

Great leaders are storytellers.

Frank Capra was born in Bisacquino, Sicily, and came to America in 1903 to write a new story for himself.

In time, it was stories written by others that Capra directed that made him one of America's most influential film directors, winning three Oscars.

In a six-year period, Capra completed *It Happened One Night*, *You Can't Take It with You*, and *Mr. Smith Goes to Washington*, receiving nominations for Best Director on each and winning the award for the first two. Following the attack on Pearl Harbor, Capra, forty-four, enlisted and was put to work producing propaganda films, including the *Why We Fight* series and *Prelude to War*, considered masterpieces of war documentaries and winning Capra two more Academy Awards.

But it was his 1946 film *It's a Wonderful Life* that has become a Christmas season classic and is considered one of the best one hundred American films ever made.

The story was conceived by historian Philip Van Doren Stern on February 12, 1938.

Stern began telling the story he called "The Greatest Gift," but no one wanted to buy the rights. "By this time," Stern remembers, "I had become fond of the story that nobody wanted." He packaged the story as a twenty-four-page booklet and sent it to friends at Christmas. A booklet found its way to RKO Pictures producer David Hempstead, who showed it to actor Cary Grant. RKO bought the film rights in 1944 for $10,000. Despite assigning writers to develop a screenplay, no scripts satisfied RKO.

Frank Capra acquired the rights from RKO on September 1, 1945, for $50,000.

> ➡ **What's your story? Would you believe it if someone else were telling it? Would it inspire you?**

When Capra read the RKO scripts, he judged that none "had the spirit of the original" and he hired writers to begin a new adaptation.

Actor Jimmy Stewart starred in Capra's *You Can't Take It with*

You and *Mr. Smith Goes to Washington*, and Capra wanted Stewart to play George Bailey. As Capra finished summarizing the story to Stewart, Capra said, "This story doesn't tell very well, does it?" to which Stewart replied, "Frank, if you want to do a movie about me committing suicide, with an angel with no wings named Clarence, I'm your boy." In truth, Stewart was grateful. "Frank really saved my career," said Stewart, who had been away from Hollywood for four-and-a-half years serving in the military during World War II. Stewart turned thirty-four during the second month of filming.

Donna Reed, ten years Stewart's junior, was an ideal match playing Stewart's wife, Mary. Capra completed the cast with his favorite actors, including Lionel Barrymore, Ward Bond, and Henry Travers.

Filming began on April 15, 1946, principal photography wrapped on July 27, and the film premiered on December 20, 1946.

By now, the storyline of *It's a Wonderful Life* is familiar: On Christmas Eve in 1945, prayers are heard in heaven for George Bailey of Bedford Falls, New York. In a series of flashbacks covering twenty-six years, we see George regularly putting others' interests ahead of his own. George delays his college plans to run the Bailey Building and Loan after his father dies. George helps others achieve their dreams while his remain unfulfilled.

As George and Mary prepare to depart on their overseas honeymoon, there's a run on the bank and all of the customers demand their deposits in cash. George and Mary quell the panic by using their honeymoon money to satisfy the depositors.

As we return to Christmas Eve in 1945, Uncle Billy heads to Henry Potter's bank to deposit $8,000 of the Bailey Building and

Loan's cash. When Billy accidentally places the money in Potter's newspaper, panic ensues as bankruptcy looms.

George turns to Potter for a loan, but Potter turns him down, smirking, "You're worth more dead than alive."

Despondent, George contemplates suicide.

> ➡ **With what regularity do you put others' interests ahead of your own?**

At his lowest moment, George Bailey's nature is to help others.

Angel Clarence Odbody comes to Earth and jumps off the bridge where George is standing, prompting George to jump in and save Clarence.

As they're drying out, Clarence tells George he's his guardian angel. "You look about like the kind of angel I'd get," George mutters, and then says, "I wish I'd never been born." Clarence grants his wish.

Clarence and George head into town. George discovers he's not recognized by anyone because he's never existed. The town and the people have changed for the worse because George was missing in their lives.

"Strange, isn't it?" Clarence asks George. "Each man's life touches so many other lives. When he isn't around he leaves an awful hole, doesn't he?"

> ➡ **How many lives have you truly touched? What stories will they tell about you when you're gone?**

Leaders make their mark on the world in ways that can be far-reaching and hugely significant yet invisible for months or years.

In the movie's final scene, George miraculously returns to Christmas Eve. As midnight approaches, George's brother Harry gives him a toast: "To George, the richest man in town!"

Two Years of Civil War Produce a New and Improved Magna Carta

How Putting New Teeth into a Charter Made It the World's Greatest Legal Document

> "The sealing of Magna Carta was an event that changed the constitutional landscape in this country and, over time, the world."
>
> **—LORD BINGHAM OF CORNHILL**

The image of King John affixing his seal to the Magna Carta beneath a giant oak on the banks of the Thames is a romanticized interpretation.

Before the foundation of liberty and justice could be laid, what happened that medieval Monday eight hundred years ago at

Runnymede was the equivalent of a shotgun marriage that sparked two years of death and destruction throughout England.

The document John accepted at Runnymede is not the Magna Carta but rather its predecessor, the Charter of the Forest. The dates that matter—two bookends in the process that created the Magna Carta—occur in September two years apart.

John found himself at Runnymede when dozens of barons decided they'd had enough from the King of England. The barons' grievances began with John's father, Henry II. For two generations—first with Henry, then with John—the kings squeezed the barons for money, pursued fruitless (and expensive) foreign wars, and did whatever they pleased whenever they pleased with no sense of justice and no end in sight.

When John lost another war in late 1214, civil war loomed. The barons demanded a meeting with John on Easter Sunday, April 19, 1215. John agreed to meet, and then broke his word.

The following week, in a tense meeting between the opposing factions, grievances were listed with the ultimatum that "unless the king immediately granted them," the barons would seek "sufficient satisfaction." John could either accept and honor the terms or risk his personal safety.

➡ **When have you not kept your word? What were the circumstances? The consequences?**

John gave his word yet again then sought a loophole.

He appealed to the Pope for support, and the Pope, firmly in the king's pocket, provided it.

Upon learning this news, the barons renounced their loyalty

to John. With John holed up in Dorset 121 miles (195 km) from London, the barons made their move. On May 17, the barons captured London, the most strategic stronghold in John's kingdom. One week later, John again was forced into negotiations.

The Articles of the Barons covered forty-nine matters, including reducing the king's inheritance, limiting military spending, and providing that a person accused of crimes could not be "victimized...except by the lawful judgment of his peers or by the law of the land." By the time John arrived at Runnymede, the list had grown to sixty-three clauses covering political, economic, legal, social, and ecclesiastical matters.

Chief among the list was a clause appointing twenty-five barons to "uphold and cause to be observed with all their might, the peace and liberties" John would soon swear to uphold. Should the king "transgress against any of the articles," the barons could "distress" the king "in all ways possible." The king would continue to have power to make laws; he now would be forced to obey them.

John agreed reluctantly.

In the time it took scribes to copy the document, John decided yet again to break his promise. By the end of July, he was chafing at the restrictions imposed on him. By August 24, he had requested and received yet again from the Pope the new treaty's annulment. On September 5, the first bookend of the Magna Carta was shoved into place when John's loyal clergymen excommunicated each baron present at Runnymede.

Civil war broke out.

➡ **How do you respond when you place your trust in someone and they let you down?**

John recruited thousands of foreign soldiers and unleashed them on his countrymen.

The king ordered the barons' property seized, and his mercenaries tortured men, raped women, and plundered villages. Describing John's ruthlessness, Roger of Wendover, a St. Albans monk, recalled that "if the day did not satisfy the malice of the king," he ordered further destruction to "refresh his sight with the damage done to his enemies."

By Christmas, John retired to Nottingham, the place infamously characterized in the legend of Robin Hood 150 years later. A more contemporary view of John twenty years after his death by Benedictine monk Mathew Paris held that "England reeks of John's filthy deeds; the foulness of Hell is defiled by John."

The New Year of 1216 began the way 1215 finished, with John's mercenaries plundering England. But by October, John was dead. The following month, his son Henry III was crowned and a reissue of the Charter of the Forest was attempted. It failed. Civil war persisted.

Not until King Louis's French army defeated the English and the Treaty of Lambeth was signed on September 20, 1217, did the second bookend fall into place and see the Charter successfully reissued. To distinguish this new, longer forty thousand-word document from its predecessors, scribes called it *magna carta libertatum* (the great charter of liberties).

The Magna Carta was revamped and reissued throughout England about every five years during Henry's fifty-six-year reign, and its principles were reconfirmed in times of national turmoil.

➡ **What program have you spearheaded that will affect your organization for years? What convinces you of your initiative's lasting impact?**

Two years of carnage produced the Magna Carta—the model for all nations aspiring to articulate and uphold the principles of liberty.

Mary Edwards Walker Relishes Roles as a Suffragist, Surgeon, and Spy

How Compassion and Courage Produced the Only Female Medal of Honor Recipient

> "You [men] are not our protectors... If you were, who would there be to protect us from?"
>
> **—MARY EDWARDS WALKER**

Mary Edwards Walker learned at an early age to dress for success.

In a sense, Mary's unconventional clothing choices foreshadowed she would become America's only female Medal of Honor recipient, the armed forces' highest commendation for bravery. Other factors contributed, but Mary attracted attention.

Alvah and Vesta Walker raised their seven children (Mary being the youngest) on a farm in Oswego, New York. Alvah and Vesta were intelligent and industrious. They were devoted Christians yet practical-minded "freethinkers" with a keen sense of right and wrong who cultivated independent thinking and encouraged their children to question the status quo and stand up for their beliefs. Homeschooling was thorough and rigorous, and work in the fields was egalitarian; women were expected to tackle whatever work a man undertook. Mary and her sisters therefore viewed dresses and petticoats as restrictive, donning instead clothing fit for their work—namely, trousers.

As America's suffragette movement gathered momentum in 1848, fifteen-year-old Mary established her "reform dress" (some called it a "costume"). "I don't wear men's clothes," she countered, "I wear my own clothes."

After completing primary school, Mary and her older sisters enrolled in nearby Falley Seminary, which emphasized social reform and bolstered Mary's convictions that standards between men and women were not only unequal but unjust.

Having developed an interest in medicine from studying her father's journals, Mary pursued a medical degree, an audacious goal given her gender. With money she earned from teaching, Mary funded her education at Syracuse Medical College, graduating as a medical doctor, the only woman in her class.

"Not only every son but every daughter," proclaimed Mary, "should be given a practical knowledge of some business whereby they can support themselves." She also believed a woman's pay should equal a man's.

➡ **What childhood experiences influence your decisions today?**

Within months of graduating, Mary married fellow Syracuse alum and doctor Albert Miller in a ceremony at which Mary wore trousers and demanded the word "obey" be stricken from the ceremony.

"How barbarous," she lectured, "the very idea of one equal promising to be the slave of another instead of both entering life's greatest drama as intelligent, equal parties."

Hardly equal, Mary came from superior stock. Albert Miller was an adulterer, and when Mary learned of his infidelity, she threw him out, though it took a decade of battling judges, double standards, and stereotypes to obtain a divorce. Her medical practice—shaky because of suspicions surrounding a female doctor—folded. Her place—and her glory—would lie in hospitals and on battlefields.

It was 1860. Lincoln had accepted his party's nomination for president. War loomed.

When it came, Mary traveled to Washington, DC, eager to offer her medical services. Her customary attire of swallowtail coat worn over trousers with a starched shirt polished off with a bow tie and top hat intrigued the press corps. Bureaucrats frowned.

Despite a shortage of trained doctors, Mary's application as an assistant medical surgeon was refused. The official reason: "lack of surgical experience." The real reason: she was a woman in a man's world. She volunteered anyway, serving in the temporary military hospital set up in the U.S. Patent Office building. She spoke her mind, challenged authority, and cared for wounded Union soldiers.

"My reason for my acts has been a strong conviction of that which I believed was right," said Mary, "I do not deserve credit for standing up to my principles for I could not do otherwise."

➡ **How would those in your organization rate your fairness and consistency when evaluating performance? Do you play favorites?**

Mary Edwards Walker was made of sterner stuff than most, but battling bureaucrats who blocked her opportunities to serve in more meaningful capacities took its toll.

Mary left Washington, DC, and began lecturing; she denounced slavery and inhumane prison conditions. She reserved her harshest criticism for doctors who amputated unnecessarily, noting that disease, infection, and malpractice claimed more men than gunfire.

Mary's compassion and sense of duty brought her back to the battlefields in 1862. Between serving at the Battle of Bull Run in August and the Battle of Fredericksburg, Mary wrote to Secretary of War Edwin Stanton requesting deployment as a spy. Stanton rejected her request, but General George Henry Thomas later dispatched Mary to spy in Northern Georgia. She was captured and spent four months in a Richmond prison before being exchanged—to her amusement—for a male Confederate surgeon.

Upon her release in August 1864, she pressed for a paid commission through letters and meetings that spilled into September, finally being awarded a paid contract as Acting Assistant Surgeon with the Ohio Fifty-Second Infantry. Mary Edwards Walker had become the Army's first female surgeon.

After the war, Generals William Tecumseh Sherman and George Henry Thomas recommended Mary for the Medal of Honor. President Andrew Johnson signed a bill awarding her the medal two weeks shy of her thirty-third birthday.

→ What would happen if your colleagues were less concerned with individual credit and more interested in accomplishing the larger objective?

The causes Mary Edwards Walker believed in were met with hostile disapproval, unjustified opposition, and fierce resistance from judges, doctors, generals, one U.S. president, and even other women.

Considered a radical by those who barred her path, she introduced reforms that outlasted them all.

Walt Disney Invites His Banker to Private Screening of *Snow White and the Seven Dwarfs*

How Risking Everything Brought an Inspired Vision to Millions

> "It's kind of fun to do the impossible."
>
> **—WALT DISNEY**

Things were going great. Walt Disney decided it was time for change.

By 1933, Disney Brothers Studio set the bar for animation. Mickey Mouse had evolved from a soundless black-and-white cartoon into a talking Technicolor character. The studio had won the Academy Award for Best Short Subject for its *Flowers and Trees* picture in the *Silly Symphony* series, and Walt Disney received an honorary award "for the creation of Mickey Mouse."

The studio's latest project—*The Three Little Pigs*—was an immediate financial, artistic, and popular success. The short film's May 27, 1933, debut—two weeks after Roosevelt closed the banks—suggested deliverance from the Great Depression gripping America: the wolf symbolized economic hardship, the pigs triumphed over adversity, and "Who's Afraid of the Big Bad Wolf?" was whistled by Americans en route to breadlines. The film would earn an Academy Award.

But Walt was restless.

His memory of distributor Charles Mintz's March 1928 betrayal was still painful. Despite the studio's successful first four years, Mintz's contractual treachery pushed the brothers to the brink of collapse with no distributor relationships, no animators, and no characters they owned. Walt made himself two promises: he would hereafter control the content his studio created, and he would drive change instead of executing someone else's plans.

Walt kept his first promise with Mickey Mouse. Within four years of Mickey's May 1928 creation, he was being marketed like a celebrity, generating $70 million in sales from forty merchandise licensees, nearly $735 million in 2018 dollars.

Walt kept his second promise with *Snow White*.

"The short subject was just a filler on any program," Walt calculated. Only a full-length animated film would achieve feature-attraction status. "We needed this new adventure," Walt recalled, "this 'kick in the pants,' to jar loose some new enthusiasm and inspiration."

➡ **What must you do to stay ahead of the pack?**

Roy and Walt Disney made a great team.

Walt viewed money as a tool, leaving financial matters to Roy. Walt was the visionary. "I found out the people who live with figures as a rule, it's postmortem, it's never ahead, it's always what happened," Walt explained. "I was always ahead."

Disney's short films were different because of Walt's vision and perfectionism, starting with an emotionally compelling story. Walt demanded seamless continuity with great gags and realistic animation.

In May 1933, as *The Three Little Pigs* debuted, Walt directed Al Lichtman of United Artists to register the title *Snow White*.

Walt was a gifted storyteller, and one afternoon he gave fifty employees a half-dollar each and sent them out for dinner. When they returned, they found Walt on a dark, empty soundstage lit by a single spotlight. For the next three hours, Walt acted out *Snow White's* entire storyline. "He was a spellbinder," said animator Joe Grant. Walt's performance moved many to tears, and others claimed that night motivated them to be their best over the next three years.

To bring *Snow White* to the screen, the studio needed what every organization requires: time, money, and people. Lots of all three.

A year was invested in developing the storyline before bringing in the writers. Walt introduced sketch artists to create storyboards that animators would then use. Each role was clearly defined.

The studio had grown to two hundred people. Walt realized he needed more and better animators to create "a certain depth and realism." On December 23, 1935, Walt's eight-page memo to

Don Graham noted that "some of our established animators at the present time are lacking in many things." Graham's pupils would need to unlearn what had brought them to the pinnacle of their career and then learn a new way of thinking and drawing. They would have to do it quickly.

"Of all the things I've done," Walt believed, "the most vital is coordinating those who work with me and aiming their efforts at a certain goal." Walt wasn't drawing, but he was doing his job. Everyone else in the studio would be expected to do theirs.

➡ **Whose job are you doing? Yours or someone else's?**

A decision to finish what you've started can be riskier—and therefore more difficult to make—than a decision to begin.

Finishing *Snow White* was a huge risk.

The premiere was set for December 21, 1937, but as late as November 1935—more than two years from its inception—the names of the seven dwarfs were not finalized. Song recordings began in January 1936, animation the following month. More than 750 artists were now working three eight-hour shifts producing the film's nearly two million images.

But time and money were running out.

Disney originally estimated *Snow White*'s cost at $250,000. Costs skyrocketed. In May 1936, Roy secured a $630,000 loan. In March 1937, he secured a $650,000 loan. *Snow White* was called *Disney's Folly* by industry insiders.

"Roy was very brave…until the costs passed over a million," Walt recalled. "When costs passed the $1.5 million mark, Roy didn't even bat an eye. He couldn't; he was paralyzed."

Finishing the project required another $327,000. As much as Walt disdained the "goddamn bankers," he needed them, and he was forced to mortgage his home. The budget was approaching $2 million, $32 million in 2018 dollars.

Walt grudgingly invited Joe Rosenberg of Bank of America to a September 14, 1937, screening to obtain final funding to finish *Snow White*. Rosenberg said little during the screening. The silence was deafening as Walt walked Rosenberg to his car. Before driving off, Rosenberg said to Walt, "That thing is going to make you a hatful of money." Walt got his money.

Snow White's premiere changed animation forever. Walt Disney had just turned thirty-six.

➡ **What's your definition of winning big? What must you do to win big?**

Snow White is ranked among the one hundred greatest American films. Walt Disney has won more Academy Awards than anyone: twenty-two Oscars from fifty-nine nominations.

Today, the Walt Disney Company is the world's largest independent media conglomerate and owns theme parks around the world.

Benjamin Franklin Convenes First Junto Club in Philadelphia

How a Group of Business Leaders Made Each Other Better

> "A man wrapped up in himself makes a very small bundle."
>
> **—BENJAMIN FRANKLIN**

It's lonely at the top.

If you're a leader, to whom can you turn for thoughtful discussions on significant matters? For fresh perspectives on thorny issues? For brutally honest feedback from peers who have only your best interests at heart? For support without repayment? For accountability without judgment?

Are you open to multiple points of view, or do you prefer examining an issue with people who think like you?

Is it fair to drag family members into these deliberations? Will they fully appreciate the stakes, the odds, and how you're feeling? Can they be impartial?

In October 1727, Benjamin Franklin invited eleven enterprising Philadelphia tradesmen to form a club for "mutual improvement" that became known as the Leather Apron Club and that was referred to by its members as the Junto.

Franklin likely modeled the Junto on an English group formed in the 1690s by philosopher John Locke and English merchants William Popple and Benjamin Furly.

Franklin's Junto met every Friday evening, and while the men certainly enjoyed one another's company, Franklin was clear from the outset the purpose of the meetings was each member's growth and development.

The distinguishing characteristics of the Junto included its middle-class orientation (society's elite already enjoyed clubs of their own); meetings were to be "conducted in the sincere spirit of inquiry after truth, without fondness for dispute, or desire for victory;" and members were required to follow rules adopted by the Junto, including asking a member to stand and place a hand over his heart and answer four questions: Do you have disrespect for any current member? Do you love mankind in general regardless of religion or profession? Do you believe people should be punished for their opinions or mode of worship? Do you love and pursue truth for its own sake?

⇒ **You're the average of the ten people with whom you spend the most time. Who are these people in your life? Are they pulling you up or dragging you down?**

Those who aspire to greatness know they need help.

Self-awareness is a necessary step toward improvement, and Franklin was honest enough with himself to recognize his growth as a person and businessman depended on those with whom he associated.

He also knew one of his faults was talking too much. His "prattling, punning, and joking" served him well as the author of *Poor Richard's Almanack*, but Franklin worried this style of conversation limited his acceptance to "trifling company."

When it became clear to Franklin that knowledge "was obtained by the use of the ear [and not] the tongue," he adopted the Socratic method of conversing, and this approach became the chosen way for issues to be discussed in the Junto. The club's rules stipulated that every member would produce topics for discussion and each member was expected to "produce and read an essay of his own writing" every three months. Topics, questions, and recommended books were posted before each meeting to guarantee rich discussions.

Franklin developed a list of standing questions to guide the discussions, including:

◆ Have you met with anything in the author you last read, remarkable, or suitable to be communicated to the Junto?

◆ Hath any citizen in your knowledge failed in his business lately, and what have you heard of the cause?

◆ Have you lately heard of any citizen's thriving well, and by what means?

◆ Do you know of any fellow citizen who has lately done a worthy action, deserving praise and imitation? Or who has committed an error proper for us to be warned against and avoid?

The other eleven hardworking members of the Junto were eager for self-improvement: a printer, a surveyor, a shoemaker, a glazier, a cabinetmaker, various other merchants, and a bartender. Iron sharpened iron as these men helped each other.

In 1743, the Junto became the American Philosophical Society and is active today.

> ⟹ **Strong leaders admit their weaknesses, fears, and failures. In what settings and with what people are you willing to be vulnerable? What's one thought you're willing to disclose this week to lift a burden you're carrying?**

U.S. president Andrew Jackson gathered his unofficial advisers in 1831 following the purge of his official cabinet after his break with Vice President John Calhoun.

Ronald Reagan assembled his "Kitchen Cabinet" of trusted friends who shared Reagan's values but who weren't afraid to tell him the truth.

Almost 230 years to the day after Franklin convened the Junto, Milwaukee business owner Bob Nourse convened a meeting of noncompeting business owners to help him solve a significant business problem. The meeting was effective, and Nourse figured other leaders would invest their time and money to join a group whose members were other business owners who, unlike consultants, brought firsthand experience to discussions.

Nourse's October 1957 meeting launched what today is Vistage International, the world's largest peer advisory board for CEOs, owners, partners, and executives.

⟶ **What significant decision must you make in the next ninety days? What's the value of gaining perspective from smart people who want nothing but your success?**

"When two men in business always agree," William Wrigley Jr. noted in 1931, "one of them is unnecessary."

Who do you trust to tell you what you need to hear?

John F. Kennedy and Nikita Khrushchev End Cuban Missile Crisis

How Learning from Mistakes Helped JFK Resolve a Cold War Conflict and Prevent World War III

> "Leadership and learning are indispensable to each other."
>
> **—JOHN F. KENNEDY**

In 1962, America and Russia hurtled toward thermonuclear annihilation.

World War II's once-allied superpowers had become lethal adversaries, each distrustful of the other's clout, motives, and saber rattling. In 1949, Russia tested its first atomic bomb. Nuclear war was a real threat.

By 1960, Nikita Khrushchev had succeeded Stalin as Soviet premier. America was in the process of deciding whether Eisenhower's vice president Richard Nixon or Senator John

F. Kennedy (JFK) would become the country's thirty-fifth president.

Kennedy attacked the administration's international track record, singling out Cuba as "the most glaring failure of American foreign policy."

In September, seventy million Americans watched Nixon and Kennedy in the first-ever televised presidential debate, inaugurating a new political era where image mattered as much as message. Kennedy's good looks and confident, relaxed manner won the night and, six weeks later, the closest presidential election in history. Television "turned the tide," Kennedy observed.

The Soviets' 1957 Sputnik launch surprised America. Space was now the benchmark for measuring nuclear supremacy. America was behind.

Kennedy's obsession with removing Cuba's Fidel Castro backfired in the disastrous Bay of Pigs invasion in April 1961. Headed into their June summit in Vienna, Khrushchev, sixty-seven, basked in a stunning triumph; Kennedy, forty-five, was bruised by a "colossal mistake." Khrushchev pressed his advantage, and Kennedy called the summit the "roughest thing in my life."

Sensing JFK's vulnerability and wanting to strengthen the Russia-Cuba relationship while deterring further U.S. invasions, Khrushchev agreed in a July 1962 secret meeting with Castro to provide Cuba missiles. By summer's end, missile installation was underway—90 miles (140 km) from Florida.

On October 15, aerial reconnaissance photos caught the Soviets red-handed. No plan existed to confront this emergency because U.S. intelligence professionals were convinced the Soviets would never make this move.

The next day at 11:45 a.m., Kennedy convened the Executive Committee of the National Security Council to determine America's response.

➡ **What significant changes have your competitors made? What steps can you take to be open-minded to marketplace disruption—no matter how unlikely?**

"How could I have been so stupid?" JFK wondered.

The Bay of Pigs failure occurred because bad ideas went unchallenged. This time, JFK would ask more questions and encourage more debate. With the ExComm assembled, Kennedy posed the first of many questions, weighing options to decide the world's fate. What were the Russians up to in Cuba? "How do you know this is a medium-range ballistic missile?" Kennedy asked.

With that question answered, others followed: When will the missiles be operational? What are our options? When do we tell our allies and what help do we want?

Generals advocated military solutions; politicians leaned toward diplomacy.

As the meeting concluded, JFK summarized the options: eliminate the missiles by land invasion or air strike; initiate a naval blockade; or leverage diplomatic pressure.

There were more questions to answer before the next meeting at 6:30 p.m.

➡ **Are you telling more than asking? What questions should you be asking about your biggest problems?**

Every option, every move was calculated.

Throughout the crisis, JFK kept his cool, even when criticized. The hawks viewed JFK as indecisive or, worse, spineless. Hardly. He was evaluating his choices. The world could not afford another Bay of Pigs. Air Force chief of staff General Curtis LeMay challenged JFK, saying "You're in a pretty bad fix."

"You're in there with me," Kennedy shot back.

JFK kept his sense of humor in the face of unimaginable tension: "I hope you all realize that there isn't enough room in the White House Bunker for all of us."

He kept his own counsel, confident the Constitution was on his side when decision time arrived.

To succeed, Kennedy's high-stakes negotiation had to convince the Russians that the United States sought a way out while emphasizing a military response was equally possible.

On Thursday, October 18, the ExComm remained divided on its move, and at 5:00 p.m. JFK met with Soviet minister Andrei Gromyko, who lectured him about the Bay of Pigs. Because a decision wasn't finalized, JFK resisted showing Gromyko the missile photos.

"Black Saturday" was the most nerve-racking of the thirteen-day crisis as the chance of nuclear war escalated. Soviet troops in Cuba shot down an American U-2 spy plane, and JFK held back his generals. Aboard a Soviet submarine in the Caribbean, cool heads prevailed as American destroyers circled above.

Kennedy decided on a blockade. It would be, JFK reflected, "one hell of a gamble" if Khrushchev didn't back down. By Sunday, the Soviets sensed their secret had been discovered. On Monday, Khrushchev learned JFK would announce the missiles' discovery and blockade in a nationally televised speech. "The thing is we were not going to unleash war," Khrushchev complained, "we just wanted to intimidate them."

JFK gave Khrushchev twenty-four hours to respond. Attorney General Robert Kennedy delivered back-channel messages to Soviet ambassador Anatoly Dobrynin, pledging not to attack Cuba if the missiles were removed.

By October 25, Khrushchev informed Kennedy the missiles would be withdrawn. World War III was averted.

> ➡ **How would you rate your negotiating skills? What can you give up to get what you want?**

"You will never know how much bad advice I received in those days," JFK said afterward.

Whether you get good advice or bad advice, the decision is yours alone.

Henry V Defeats the Odds, Leading His Army to Victory at Agincourt

How a Small Band of Brothers Won the Day over Numerically Superior Forces

> "From this day to the ending of the world, But we in it shall be remembered—We few, we happy few, we band of brothers."
>
> **—WILLIAM SHAKESPEARE, *HENRY V***

At some point in every leader's career, there's a major battle to be fought.

After William the Conqueror invaded England from Normandy in 1066, the kings of England and France claimed each other's lands as theirs. The Battle of Agincourt was fought on October 25, 1415, to settle these claims.

The French army totaled thirty-six thousand men. "The number of them was really terrifying," an English eyewitness recounted.

The English army totaled six thousand men.

On the eve of battle, English victory seemed improbable to everyone but King Henry V. Henry had invaded France in August, three days after turning twenty-nine.

His army conquered Harfleur, but the siege took weeks longer than expected.

Henry now took his first risk, leading his army 168 miles (271 km) to Calais on a march that opened the English to French attack. As the march began, Henry stipulated that the small army must stay together. The battle that mattered was with the King of France, so men who were caught wandering off to plunder, capture prisoners for ransom, or pursue chivalric dreams would be put to death.

The two-week march was miserable. The men endured "filthy, wet, and windy weather." The English arrived at Agincourt to find their route to Calais blocked by the French. By the eve of the battle, the English were tired, wet, hungry, and sick. That night, the heavens unleashed a torrential downpour.

Undeterred, Henry ordered knights to scout the battlefield by moonlight. The scouting party confirmed the enemy's size.

Facing an unfulfilled campaign plus a daunting military challenge, Henry had three options: return to England; delay the battle to rest his men, though doing so would deflate morale and allow more French soldiers to arrive; or take the fight to the French. Henry chose to attack.

> ⇒ **When was the last time you faced long odds to achieve a significant objective? What did you learn from that experience that will help you when facing comparable risks in the future?**

Outnumbered six to one, Henry nevertheless enjoyed seven advantages.

First, the French nobles at Agincourt detested one another. Their personal, political, and territorial enmity meant they hated each other more than the English. Leading troops into battle was a badge of chivalry, and the French could not agree who would lead and who would follow. They reached a catastrophic consensus: every nobleman would lead the battle, leaving their soldiers beyond the vanguard leaderless.

Second, with the battlefield recently plowed, rain that was cursed the night before became a blessing to Henry's army. The French would be advancing toward the English through claylike mud.

Third, Henry defied military convention that "those who march lose and those who remain standing still and holding firm win." Henry's decision to attack surprised the French.

Fourth, Henry's gamble to move his battle lines forward meant the battlefield was now bracketed by dense woodlands with no way for the French to attack the English from the sides. Henry's move forced the French into the very position they wanted to avoid: frontal exposure to Henry's archers.

Fifth, the English army, though outnumbered, possessed the better leader. The men were better disciplined, and, because they believed their cause was just and their leader God-fearing, they were passionate about their mission. "Bravery," wrote Roman military expert Vegetius, one thousand years earlier, "is of more value than numbers."

Sixth, five thousand of Henry's six thousand men were archers armed with longbows. In France, archery was considered a lower-class pursuit, but English noblemen, including Henry, were expected to master the longbow. The longbow enabled Henry's archers to fire twenty arrows a minute at a great distance with armor-piercing force, killing nearly five thousand French soldiers in the first wave of the French attack.

Seventh, the size of the French army worked against the French. Soldiers in the third rank were too tightly packed to use their swords; those in the first rank who fell impeded the progress of the others. Knights wearing sixty pounds of armor who stumbled had difficulty rising to fight, and some drowned in their helmets.

➡ **How can you turn your competitors' advantages against them?**

Henry's decision to attack was based on knowing his men, understanding the battle conditions, and believing the longbow provided an advantage.

Shakespeare's depiction of the Battle of Agincourt in his 1599 play *Henry V* portrays Henry as a man of the people leading his men into battle for a just cause. Henry recalls previous victories by English kings over the French while expressing confidence the Battle of Agincourt will end in victory for the English.

King Henry V led his troops into battle and fought alongside them in hand-to-hand combat. The French king stayed behind in his palace in Paris.

⇒ Words inspire; deeds transform. How can you work alongside your colleagues to transform their actions?

In a battle lasting about three hours, Henry's army defeated a numerically superior force.

French chivalry died on Agincourt's battlefield that day, and Henry's victory ushered in a new era of power for Britain in which Henry married the French king's daughter and their son became heir to the throne of France and England.

Sir Ernest Shackleton Gives Order to "Abandon Ship"

How Abandoning Ship Did Not Mean Abandoning Hope on this Failed Antarctic Expedition

> "Loneliness is the penalty of leadership, but the man who has to make the decisions is assisted greatly if he feels that there is no uncertainty in the minds of those who follow him, and that his orders will be carried out confidently and in expectation of success."
>
> **—ERNEST SHACKLETON**

June in Antarctica is winter.

And in June 1915, British explorer Sir Ernest Shackleton and his crew were trapped in their ship *Endurance*, frozen solid in ice just off the coast of Antarctica.

The story has been told and retold—but likely is more legend than fact—that Shackleton wrote and placed an ad in *The Times* of London advertising for men to join him on his journey to the bottom of the world:

Men Wanted for Hazardous Journey. Small wages, bitter cold, long months of complete darkness, constant danger, safe return doubtful. Honor and recognition in case of success.

What is known for certain is that Shackleton and twenty-seven men had said goodbye to the sun and suffered from the −23°F (−30°C) temperatures. Now they found themselves in dire straits.

On October 27, Shackleton gave the order to abandon ship. "After long months of ceaseless anxiety and strain," Shackleton wrote, "we have been compelled to abandon the ship... The task is to reach land with all the members of the Expedition."

Shackleton's British Trans-Antarctic Expedition found itself 1,800 miles (2,897 km) from civilization with three lifeboats, meager provisions, and no means of communication. In his private diary, Shackleton wrote, "I pray God I can manage to get the whole party to civilization."

In his 1922 book *The Worst Journey in the World*, Apsley Cherry-Garrard, a contemporary of Shackleton's, wrote, "For a joint scientific and geographical piece of organisation, give me Scott; for a Winter Journey, Wilson; for a dash to the Pole and nothing else, Amundsen: and if I am in the devil of a hole and want to get out of it, give me Shackleton every time."

Shackleton learned as a young seaman that unhappy, unproductive, and disloyal staff make hard work harder. There was no question his men possessed skill and courage. But what about their character? "The personnel of an expedition," Shackleton wrote, "is a factor on which success depends to a very large extent. The men selected…must be able to live together in harmony for a long period without outside communication, and it must be remembered that the men whose desires lead them to the untrodden paths of the world have generally marked individuality."

➡ How intentional are you about hiring and promoting people based on their character? How can you be sure their values are congruent with yours? How do they respond to adversity?

Once the decision was made to abandon ship, Shackleton established routines, rotated jobs, and abolished special privileges. He knew a physically active crew would sustain morale and foster teamwork. The change in jobs combatted monotony while having the pragmatic effect of preparing one man to do another's job if worse came to worst.

He also knew double standards would erode morale and diminish others' trust in him. Shackleton did not mince words on describing their predicament, but his optimism inspired his men. Shackleton led skits, singing, and the first Antarctic Derby. With five teams competing, Second Mate Frank Wild's dog team won the seven-hundred-yard race. All twenty-eight men placed bets, and winnings were paid in chocolate and cigarettes. "Optimism," said Shackleton, "is true moral courage."

Outwardly optimistic, truthful up to a point, Shackleton nevertheless shielded his men from his darkest fears. It is yet another mark of leadership determining which of your thoughts to share and which ones you'll keep private.

As *Endurance* sank into the sea, Shackleton saw his dream of crossing the Antarctic continent sink with it. He faced more than failure. He faced death. He abandoned ship, but he did not abandon hope. How you address failure when it occurs in your world is the determining factor for your next outcome.

Shackleton was realistic, pragmatic, and determined to achieve the new objective he set for himself: get every man back to Britain safely. "A man," said Shackleton, "must shape himself to a new mark directly the old one goes to ground."

➡ **How do you know when to rely on your drive, stamina, and persistence to press forward, and when to accept defeat, adapt, and focus on a new goal?**

Shackleton's decisions saved lives.

He abandoned ship. He established a series of camps on ice floes over a six-month period. Most dangerous of all, Shackleton set sail with five men on a twenty-six-day voyage to South Georgia, 800 miles (1,287 km) from their final camp in the most storm-swept waters of the world. He was forty-one years old.

The decision Shackleton made—to save his crew, not the mission—and the new risks he took paid off.

On August 30, 1916—four and a half months after leaving his men behind on Elephant Island—the remaining twenty-two crew members were rescued. "Superhuman effort," said Shackleton, "isn't worth a damn unless it achieves results."

➡ **How much of your success has been based on favorable economic or industry climates? When was the last time you pushed yourself to accomplish something grand?**

"Leadership is a fine thing," said Shackleton, "but it has its penalties. And the greatest penalty is loneliness."

George Washington Bids Farewell to His Troops

How Saying "Goodbye" Opened New Opportunities

> "With a heart full of love and gratitude, I now take leave of you."
>
> **—GEORGE WASHINGTON**

Saying goodbye can be difficult.

For those who have not yet achieved their dream, a belief that the best is yet to come emboldens many to stay too long. For those at the top of their game, departing can seem premature.

George Washington said goodbye as commander-in-chief, as president of the Constitutional Convention, and as president of the United States.

Acutely aware his every move, word, and decision would be

judged by posterity, Washington set masterful examples for today's leaders for stepping aside.

George Washington was a born leader. His bravery, strength, stamina, and above-average height (6' 2", 1.88 m) marked him as a battlefield commander.

Arriving at the second Continental Congress in full military uniform, Washington showed he was prepared for war. Upon his unanimous election as the budding nation's commander-in-chief, Washington's brief acceptance speech was remarkable for its humility ("I do not think myself equal to the Command I am honored with") and willing self-sacrifice (advising Congress he would serve without pay).

While not a shrewd strategist, Washington's leadership was unequaled, and his wartime leadership foreshadowed his approach to leading in peacetime. He was a keen judge of talent, recruiting capable officers and then trusting those under his immediate command to do their jobs. He was practical, harboring no illusions about the ragtag army he commanded and understanding America's best hope for winning the war was outlasting the British. And he always acted on principle, dismantling internal uprisings by appealing to a higher purpose and executing British spies and American deserters with equal dispatch.

With the war successfully concluded, word of the treaty ratified in Paris reached the colonies in early November 1783. Washington was eager to resign his commission and return home.

On November 2 near Princeton, New Jersey, Washington bid farewell to soldiers of the Continental army, addressing them as "one patriotic band of brothers."

His most emotional farewell occurred on December 4 at

Fraunces Tavern in New York. Washington arrived for the noon luncheon in his best blue and buff uniform and found the tavern packed with his officers. At Washington's signal, the men began eating. Washington's heart swelled as the last glass of brandywine was poured. He swallowed hard and offered this toast: "With a heart filled with love and gratitude, I now take leave of you. I most devoutly wish that your latter days may be as prosperous and happy as your former ones have been glorious and honorable." The men raised their glasses and "tears...filled every eye."

Washington resigned his commission to Congress nineteen days later. King George III called Washington "the greatest character of the age" because of his voluntary resignation of power.

> ⟹ **How will you know when it's time for you to go?**

Washington was exhausted by the war and longed to live out his days at Mount Vernon.

His respite was short-lived.

Virginia's governor invited Washington to lead the delegates at the Constitutional Convention in Philadelphia in May 1787. Washington was loathe to accept the invitation, noting he had taken "leave of all the employments of public life." Washington also had given his word. What's more, Washington knew the Constitution required more than revising—it required overhauling. Consensus appeared elusive. Acutely aware of his legacy, and characterizing the current government "like a house on fire," Washington wanted nothing to do with failure.

On the other hand, presiding over a favorable outcome would secure his place in history.

Once James Madison convinced Washington that the majority of the delegates favored the constitutional transformation, Washington agreed to participate.

Arriving in Philadelphia, Washington was elected unanimously to preside over the Constitutional Convention. Though he spoke little during the proceedings, Washington's influence was profound.

> ➡ **You've achieved every major goal you sought to accomplish. You're ready to go. How will you respond if you're asked to stay?**

With the Constitution ratified, Washington again sought retirement. Instead, all sixty-nine electors voted for Washington to become the nation's first president. It was his third unanimous election to lead.

Walking "on untrodden ground," Washington once again proved himself an able leader, defining the role of the presidency and creating the government. He established a presidential cabinet; appointed the entire Supreme Court; satisfied all debts; created a national bank; implemented an effective tax system; and took personal control over the ten-square-mile federal district, including the President's mansion and the Capitol on the banks of the Potomac.

As the presidential election of 1792 approached, Washington planned yet again to retire rather than seek a second term. By this time, Jefferson and Hamilton were in such open disagreement, "the only issue on which Jefferson and Hamilton could apparently agree is Washington's indispensability."

On February 13, 1793, the electoral college unanimously elected Washington to another four-year term that Washington described to Jefferson as "the extreme wretchedness of his existence."

> ➡ **What did you give to your career beyond your time? What did you receive in return? What will be your legacy?**

On September 19, 1796, Washington's farewell address was printed in newspapers, notifying the nation he declined to be "considered among the number of those out of whom a choice is to be made" for the next president. His last day in office was March 4, 1797, voluntarily resigning as the young nation's first president.

George Washington died December 14, 1799, at age sixty-seven, after catching a cold while riding around Mount Vernon on horseback in freezing rain, snow, and hail. His retirement had lasted less than two years. On his deathbed, in a voice barely audible to those gathered around him, Washington said, "Doctor, I die hard, but I am not afraid to go."

A grieving nation bid a final farewell to George Washington on December 26, 1799, remembering this great soldier and statesman as "first in war, first in peace, and first in the hearts of his countrymen."

Herbert Hoover Designates a Permanent Place for Relaxing

How Even the Busiest Executive Made Time for R & R

> "Presidents have only two moments of personal seclusion. One is prayer; the other is fishing—and they cannot pray all the time!"
>
> **—HERBERT HOOVER**

Within days of his November 6, 1928, landslide election as president of the United States, Herbert Hoover made a decision that's been upheld by each of his successors.

Hoover was not absorbed by military matters, though Marines would soon figure into his decision. Hoover's thinking had no bearing on his domestic agenda nor on foreign policy. Rather, he realized he'd need a nearby reprieve from the "pneumatic hammer" beating on him as the nation's chief executive. He also required relief from the swampy, humid site that George Washington selected for the nation's capital.

Clark Clifford, adviser to presidents Truman, Kennedy, Johnson, and Carter, noted, "If every weekend you had to stay in the White House, after a while you would have men in white coats walking around."

George Washington retreated to Mount Vernon, Thomas Jefferson to Monticello—locations reasonably close to the capital. Hoover established America's first presidential retreat because his adopted state of California was too distant for regular getaways. He directed Lawrence Richey to find a place within 100 miles (161 km) of the capital that had 2,500 feet (762 m) of elevation for cooler temperatures; was mosquito-free; featured plenty of woods for hiking and privacy; and had a mountain view and fishing streams.

Richey had served Hoover twelve years and knew the Hoover family's love of the outdoors, particularly Hoover's fondness for fishing. Richey knew, too, that Hoover's communion with Mother Nature reenergized him—and the new president would need every ounce of energy that he could muster during his four difficult years in office.

Within sixty days of Hoover's election, Richey recommended several sites for consideration. First Lady Lou Henry Hoover and Herbert Hoover visited these sites on January 20, 1929, and then selected Doubletop Mountain alongside the Rapidan River in Virginia's Shenandoah Valley. By mid-April, private funds were raised to purchase approximately 164 acres.

Hoover would spend hundreds of days at Rapidan Camp.

> ➡ **When did you last fully unplug from your office? What must you do to enable your team to run the office for at least two weeks without you?**

Constructing Hoover's camp was a job for the Marines.

Within weeks of Hoover's site selection, nearly one hundred Marines commanded by Major Earl Long began clearing brush, blasting rock, and carving roads. "With one exception," Long noted, "this was the most difficult task in my career as an engineer, covering about twenty-three years."

One hundred eighteen days after selecting the site, Hoover slept in one of the camp's five tents.

Hoover refused money that Congress allocated to construct the camp and rejected funds appropriated by Virginia's legislature, paying for the improvements himself. The roads developed for Rapidan Camp were constructed with local and state interests in mind.

On August 17, 1929, the camp opened to the public and hundreds flocked to the site.

Upon learning no school existed in the remote location, Hoover funded the construction of a schoolhouse and the lone teacher's salary.

Hoover tamed Madison County's wilderness but could not tame the Great Depression, and he was soundly defeated by Franklin D. Roosevelt in 1932. Before leaving office, Hoover donated Rapidan Camp to the National Park Service.

Hoover's generosity was unknown to most Americans.

> ⇒ **How are you using your position to provide for those less fortunate than you? What else could you do?**

When FDR succeeded Hoover and visited Rapidan, he found the narrow trails too rough for his wheelchair and the mountain streams too cold for swimming.

Roosevelt preferred sailing, but the Secret Service prohibited this activity, fearful of German submarine activity. FDR asked the National Park Service director to survey new sites within a one-hundred-mile radius of the capital.

Roosevelt's New Deal had unleashed dozens of public works projects, including the development of the Catoctin Recreational Demonstration Area program near Thurmont, Maryland. On April 22, 1942, FDR selected this site as his presidential retreat. On August 8, 1942, FDR's first full day on-site, six German saboteurs who'd come ashore from Nazi submarines were executed, confirming the wisdom of forbidding presidential yachting.

FDR named the camp Shangri-La and visited often, though the exact location was not disclosed for security reasons. FDR hosted Winston Churchill and extended invitations to staff members and officials as political perks.

FDR's successor Harry Truman seldom visited, but Eisenhower loved the place, renaming it Camp David to honor his father and grandson. He built a three-hole golf course on the property. Ike held the first cabinet meeting at Camp David and hosted British Prime Minister Harold Macmillan and Soviet premier Nikita Khrushchev.

Each U.S. president has utilized Camp David to varying degrees; all recognized the camp's effect to relax tensions and change the context for important discussions—whether with trusted advisers, domestic politicians, or world leaders.

Serious meetings held in relaxed settings allow participants to access different parts of their hearts and minds and consider new possibilities.

"To me," said Lady Bird Johnson, "Camp David is more a psychological journey than a physical one."

➡ **What major problem or opportunity would benefit from gathering key people and moving the discussion from the office to a more relaxing venue?**

The greater the responsibility, the greater the need for a refuge.

Viktor Frankl Tests His Theory on Himself in a Concentration Camp

How the Power of Purpose Was Galvanized in a Nazi Death Camp

"Everything can be taken from a man but one thing: the last of the human freedoms—to choose one's attitude in any given set of circumstances, to choose one's own way."
—VIKTOR FRANKL

As war approached, two men would come to symbolize to the world the vast chasm separating abject evil from love's selfless vulnerability:

Joseph Goebbels, Reich Minister of Propaganda of Nazi Germany and virulent anti-Semite, and Viktor Frankl, renowned psychiatrist and son of devout Jews Elsa and Gabriel Frankl.

To be Jewish in Germany as Adolf Hitler came to power in 1933 was to face great professional, financial, and personal risk. Though Jews represented less than one percent of Germany's total population, Hitler blamed them for all of the country's problems: its World War I defeat, rampant inflation, the spread of Bolshevism. Pressure on Jews mounted under Hitler. Their businesses were boycotted and they were banned from holding university and civil service positions. The 1935 Nuremberg Laws rescinded Jews' German citizenship. In 1936, a special tax was levied on Jews. By 1937, Nazis were pressuring German businesses to fire their Jewish employees. By 1938, Jews were being rounded up and deported.

On November 3, 1938, Herschel Grynszpan received an impassioned postcard in Paris from his parents who'd been deported to Poland from Germany. On November 7, Grynszpan walked into Germany's Paris embassy and shot diplomat Ernst vom Rath.

On November 9, 1938—twenty years to the day when the Allies presented harsh terms for Germany's World War I surrender—vom Rath died and Goebbels seized the moment, casting vom Rath's death as a nationwide Jewish plot.

That evening, Goebbels unleashed a pogrom unprecedented in European history: *Kristallnacht* (Night of Broken Glass) became the Holocaust's first act. The glass destroyed that night equaled half the yearly production of Belgian glass manufacturers.

By dawn, more than 275 synagogues lay in ashes, 7,500 Jewish businesses had been destroyed, thousands of homes had been sacked, dozens of prominent Jews had been murdered, and hundreds more had been collected for shipment to concentration camps.

⮕ **What throws you out of balance? How do you handle adversity? What has adversity taught you?**

Viktor Frankl entered medical school as Hitler began writing *Mein Kampf* from prison in 1924.

Frankl's pioneering work counseling people with suicidal tendencies raised his profile, and he was invited to deliver the keynote address at the International Congress for Individual Psychology. He was twenty-one years old. Frankl continued this work after graduating and in 1937 established his Viennese practice in neurology and psychiatry in the face of Nazi hardships and restrictions.

Shortly before Pearl Harbor—nearly three years to the day after Goebbels ordered Kristallnacht—Frankl received word that a visa awaited him at the American Consulate in Vienna. The visa was for Frankl only. He was torn: *Could I really afford to leave my parents alone to face their fate, to be sent, sooner or later, to a concentration camp? Where did my responsibility lie?*

While discussing this dilemma with his father, Frankl noticed a marble fragment on a table, and Frankl's father explained that he'd picked it up from the ashes of Vienna's largest synagogue following Kristallnacht. It was from one of the Ten Commandments. "Which one?" Viktor asked.

"Honor they father and mother."

That "hint from Heaven" sealed Viktor's decision. He would stay with his parents in Vienna despite the certainty that a concentration camp lay in their future. On September 24, 1942, Viktor Frankl, his wife, the rest of his family, and fifteen hundred other Jews were herded into freight cars bound for Theresienstadt.

Upon arrival at the death camp, Frankl and his family were separated. Frankl was stripped of everything except his glasses, a belt, and his shoes. He was now prisoner number 119104. He was thirty-six years old.

Ninety percent of those arriving were sent to gas chambers. During the first few days in camp, Frankl recalled, "most of us were overcome with a grim sense of humor." Humor became the initial coping mechanism.

> ➡ When things are bad, leaders acknowledge the truth while putting themselves and others at ease. What tension is occurring in your organization that humor could relieve?

During medical school, Frankl developed a new approach to psychiatry.

Sigmund Freud believed a person's behavior resulted from subconscious thoughts. Alfred Adler believed a person's whole environment determined their behavior. Frankl coined the term "logotherapy": the belief that striving to find meaning in one's life is the most powerful motivating force in human beings.

In the death camps, Frankl tested his theory on himself.

Frankl watched many fellow prisoners turn to their past to blunt the "terrible and immense horror" of the camps. "The prisoner who had lost faith in the future—his future—was doomed," he wrote in *Man's Search for Meaning*. That person would lose their "spiritual hold," becoming susceptible to "mental and physical decay." For them, life "became meaningless."

During his imprisonment, Frankl realized "man...can only live by looking to the future." So Frankl pictured in his mind "giving a lecture on the psychology of the concentration camp."

That powerful motivating force allowed Frankl to endure the horrors of Dachau until American soldiers liberated the camp on April 27, 1945.

> ➡ Where do you find meaning in your life? What principle, cause, value, or purpose would you be willing to defend to the death or devote your life to pursuing? Why?

Viktor Frankl's *Man's Search for Meaning* is regarded as one of the most influential books written and has sold more than ten million copies.

Nelson Mandela Opens Anti-Apartheid Talks from Prison

How Confidence and Humility Paved the Way for Forgiveness and Healing

> "Courageous people do not fear forgiving, for the sake of peace."
>
> **—NELSON MANDELA**

For as long as humans have walked the earth, someone's been in charge.

We're pack animals, naturally looking to dominant group members to lead. Great leaders help others become better while striving toward something grander than a single person can achieve alone.

Others in authority, however, abuse their power to control people for personal gain. Every organization has jerks, but if you work for one, you're paid a salary and are free to leave anytime you wish. Slavery is outlawed in all recognized countries, yet servitude—arranged marriages, domestic servants held captive, child laborers—is more prevalent than at any time in history.

In South Africa's 1948 national election, Daniel François Malan became prime minister running on a platform of "apartness"—*apartheid* in Afrikaans.

The Prohibition of Mixed Marriages Act of 1949 was followed by the Immorality Act, laws making it illegal for South Africans to marry or pursue sexual relationships across racial lines. The Population Registration Act classified all South Africans into one of four racial groups—"black," "white," "coloured," and "Indian"— and residential communities were determined by these classifications. From 1960 to 1983, 3.5 million nonwhite South Africans were uprooted and forced into segregated neighborhoods in one of modern history's largest mass relocations.

Nelson Mandela was twenty-four years old when Malan was elected. He viewed this oppression as "a monolithic system that was diabolical in its detail, inescapable in its reach, and overwhelming in its power."

Mandela earned his undergraduate degree from University College of Fort Hare and his law degree from the University of the Witwatersrand, where he was the only black student and experienced racism. In 1942, Mandela joined the African National Congress (ANC) and two years later cofounded its Youth League—organizations dedicated to overthrowing apartheid.

Mandela's intelligence, diligence, and focus impressed his ANC peers, and in 1950 Mandela was elected to ANC's National Executive Committee.

➡ **Do people follow you because they're obligated to do so or because they're inspired? How can you be sure?**

Even before his election as an ANC leader, Mandela was leading.

In 1949, he encouraged the ANC to mobilize South Africans against apartheid through nonviolent protests such as boycotts, strikes, and other civil disobedience initiatives. The protests placed participants at risk since striking was illegal.

Mandela appreciated his responsibility, and he "had to weigh arguments and make decisions, and expect to be criticized by rebels like myself."

On June 26, 1952, thousands participated in a National Day of Protest, and from that day forward Mandela was a marked man: he was forced to resign his ANC membership, prohibited from traveling outside Johannesburg, and barred from attending organized meetings. In August 1952, Mandela opened his law firm with Oliver Tambo, becoming the first black law firm in Johannesburg. They dedicated themselves to providing legal assistance to Africans accused of violating apartheid laws.

In June 1955, ANC chapters throughout South Africa sent three thousand delegates to a Congress of the People. In December 1956, Mandela was arrested and charged with treason, a crime punishable by death.

Mandela's trial would begin in August 1959. Leaving his family, Mandela took advantage of not being jailed to work underground, visiting foreign countries, raising funds, and building opposition against apartheid. At home, he traveled disguised as a chauffeur. On August 5, 1960, Mandela was arrested while traveling from Durban to Johannesburg.

At his trial, Mandela testified, "I was made, by the law, a criminal, not because of what I had done, but because of what I stood for."

His life was spared, but he was sentenced to life imprisonment.

➡ **When have you paid a price to honor your principles? What price did you pay? Would you make the same decision again?**

Mandela spent nearly three decades behind bars.

"Prison," he wrote, "is designed to break one's spirit and destroy one's resolve."

On Robben Island, 4.3 miles (6.9 km) off the coast of Cape Town, South Africa, Mandela was held in a damp concrete cell measuring 8 feet (2.4 m) by 7 feet (2.1 m) with a straw mat for sleeping. He was sentenced to labor in the quarry.

Twenty-one years passed, but Mandela did not break.

On November 23, 1985, Mandela was discharged from Volks Hospital following prostate surgery and taken to Pollsmoor Prison. He seized the opportunity that the "solitude" provided, having "concluded that the time had come when the struggle could best be pushed forward through negotiations. If we did not start a dialogue soon, both sides would be plunged into a dark night of oppression."

Without informing the ANC, Mandela wrote to the South African government encouraging peace talks.

Over the next four and a half years, Mandela led negotiations with the government. He was released on February 11, 1990, and asked about his anger toward whites. "I had none," Mandela said.

He viewed whites as "fellow South Africans" and he wanted them to know "we appreciate the contribution that they have made toward the development of this country."

South Africa's first multiracial elections were held April 27, 1994. Mandela won with 62 percent of the votes and was inaugurated on May 10, 1994, as the country's first black president. He was seventy-six.

Mandela invited his jailer Christo Brand to the inauguration, later naming him to a post in his administration.

➡ **Who do you need to forgive?**

Nelson Mandela and F. W. de Klerk won the 1993 Nobel Peace Prize for abolishing apartheid in South Africa.

Sam Walton Hires His First Partner to Support Aggressive Expansion Plan

How a Willingness to Share Profits Made Sam Walton America's Richest Man

> "If everybody is doing it one way, there's a good chance you can find your niche by going exactly in the opposite direction."
>
> **—SAM WALTON**

Entrepreneurs joke that they start their businesses not only because they believe they can offer customers something they're not getting, but because they can't work for someone else.

Sam Walton was such an entrepreneur.

When Walton left the Army in 1945, he knew two things: he wanted to work in retail, and he didn't want to work for someone else.

With a loan from his father-in-law, Walton purchased a Ben Franklin variety store franchise in Newport, Arkansas, for $25,000. Describing it as "a real dog," Walton nevertheless vowed his new store would "be the best, most profitable variety store in Arkansas within five years."

Knowing little about retailing, Walton relied on home office manuals describing effective store operations. It wasn't long, though, before Walton began breaking the rules: devising promotional programs, buying direct from wholesalers, and eliminating the home office's 25 percent middleman fee.

Sam Walton's vision for what would become the world's largest retailer was coming into focus: operate in small towns and sell merchandise at the lowest possible prices.

In two and a half years, Walton repaid the loan and annual sales jumped to $175,000 from $75,000. The turnaround was achieved by hard work and observing the competition. "I learned a lesson," said Walton. "You can learn from everybody."

Then disaster struck.

Walton's landlord had watched the store's turnaround, and refused to renew the lease. He wanted the store for himself.

It became the low point of Walton's business career. He'd worked hard but failed to read the contract's fine print.

"It's not just a corny saying that you can make a positive out of most any negative if you work at it hard enough," says Walton. "The challenge at hand was simple enough to figure out: I had to pick myself up and get on with it, do it all over again, only even better this time." He was thirty-one years old.

➡️ **What is the foremost challenge of your organization—and therefore your primary responsibility to address?**

Walton located another store available for purchase in Bentonville, Arkansas, 220 miles (354 m) away.

Walton used $50,000 from selling the Newport store to purchase his new Bentonville store, which opened on July 29, 1950, as Walton's Five and Dime, even though it was a Ben Franklin franchise store.

Despite Bentonville's reluctance to welcome newcomers, Sam Walton's energy was irresistible. The store became an immediate success; sales doubled in two years.

"Mr. Walton just had a personality that drew people in," remembers Inez Threet, who worked there. "He would just yell [hello] at everybody he saw, and that's the reason so many liked him and did business in the store."

In 1954, Walton opened a store with his brother James Lawrence "Bud" Walton in Ruskin, Missouri. Expansion fever necessitated two key investments.

The first investment was an Ercoupe airplane purchased secondhand for $1,850 in April 1954, which didn't "even look like an airplane," said Bud, who'd been a Navy pilot. But it saved Walton countless hours scouting locations.

The second investment was more difficult and required creativity. Sam Walton needed people he could count on to execute his plans. His biggest hiring move was convincing Bob Bogle to become his first manager.

Walton had approached Bogle a couple of times, and Bogle hadn't been interested. Walton—wary of partners yet a keen judge of people—invited Bob and his wife, Marilyn, over to his home one evening and showed them the books, shared his plans, and offered Bogle 25 percent of the store's profits.

Marilyn "was pretty sure I'd lost my mind," Bogle recalls. She didn't want him to leave his state health inspector's job, but Bogle said his current job promised no upside.

"It seemed like a good opportunity," said Bogle, "and the thing that fascinated me more than the salary was the opportunity to buy an interest in the other stores as we put them in."

It was December 1, 1955, and Sam Walton had hired his first lieutenant. Bogle, twenty-nine, worked for Walton the rest of his career. He coined the name Walmart, keeping Walton in the name and figuring "it's only got seven letters and I know how much [those letters] cost."

Walton's creative approach to sharing profits kick-started expansion. By 1970, Walton had seventy-eight partners.

> ⇒ **Do your people believe the organization is moving in the right direction? What would inspire top talent to work here?**

Sam Walton had a passion for saving customers money and a bias for action.

"There is only one boss: the customer," insisted Walton. "And he can fire everybody in the company from the chairman on down, simply by spending his money somewhere else."

So Sam Walton was constantly searching for the next idea, taking them from competitors, customers, and colleagues.

One idea—hatched in 1962—became the backbone of the company's culture.

If store associates had to work on Saturdays, then Walmart executives would, too. Sales figures, trendy merchandise, and key mistakes were shared, giving Walmart a two-day head start over adjustments that competitors would make on Monday.

"If you don't want to work weekends," said Walton, "you shouldn't be in retail."

➡ **What time of day are you most productive? How can you reserve more time at the peak of your productivity?**

In 1982, *Forbes* named Walton the richest man in America.

Today, Walmart is the world's largest company by revenue and the largest private employer with more than 2.3 million employees.

Marie Curie Defies the Royal Swedish Academy of Sciences

How the Two-Time Nobel Prize Winner's Courage and Dignity Shined through Scandal

> "Life is not easy for any of us. But what of that? We must have perseverance and above all confidence in ourselves. We must believe that we are gifted for something and that this thing must be attained."
>
> **—MARIE CURIE**

Bronisława and Władysław Skłodowski prepared their children for extraordinary lives.

Doing so required considerable effort. Tsarist Russia ruled Poland in 1863. Significant leadership posts were unavailable to Poles. The Russians—intent on suppressing Polish nationalism to "kill the soul of a people"—forbid the teaching of Polish history, philosophy, and literature; many Poles secretly defied their occupiers, risking banishment to Siberia.

Bronisława obtained an advanced education—a rare accomplishment—and became headmistress of a prestigious girls' school, a position she held until shortly after her fifth child was born. Władysław taught math and physics. When the Russians banned these subjects, Władysław brought home the laboratory equipment, conveying to his children the joy of experimentation and discovery. Maria, the youngest, was most interested and later became Marie Curie, the first woman awarded a Nobel Prize and the only woman twice honored.

The Skłodowski children learned eagerly. Maria was the family constellation's brightest star, reading at age four and placing first in all subjects despite being two years younger than her classmates.

Władysław's rebuke of his Russian supervisor cost him his job, forcing him from his lodgings and into lower paying jobs. Hardship became heartbreak when the oldest child died of tuberculosis at fourteen; Bronisława died from tuberculosis two years later at forty-two. The children, though devastated, were nevertheless imbued with "an invincible force."

Upon receiving a gold medal for graduating first in her class, Maria and her sister Bronia enrolled in Poland's Flying University, a clandestine women's institution for whom higher education was forbidden.

Despite hardship, the Skłodowskis raised a teacher, two doctors, and a Nobel laureate.

➡ To what extent do your employees demonstrate a desire
to learn, improve, and increase their value? To own
their careers? What's your approach to mentoring your
employees?

Maria and her older sister made a pact: Bronia would travel
to Paris to continue her education and, once established, would
summon Maria.

For the next four years while serving as a governess, Maria
educated herself, reading books on physics, anatomy, and sociol-
ogy in Polish, Russian, and French.

Joining her now-married sister in Paris in November 1891,
Maria became one of 210 women among the Sorbonne's more
than nine thousand students. Maria—now calling herself
Marie—excelled in school, obtaining her *licence ès sciences* in
1893 (finishing first), and her *licence ès mathématiques* in 1894
(finishing second).

During spring of 1894, Marie was introduced to Pierre Curie,
who had access to larger laboratory space that Marie required. Like
Marie, Pierre was a prodigy, publishing his first scientific paper,
with his brother, at age twenty.

On July 26, 1895, Pierre and Marie were married.

For the next two years, they pursued their own research. In
December 1897, Pierre dropped his projects to collaborate with
Marie. More than husband and wife, they were equal partners.

On July 13, 1898, they discovered polonium, which they
named for Marie's Poland. Their joint paper introduced a new
term: "radioactive."

The Curies received a letter in November 1903 congratulating them on winning the Nobel Prize. Though Marie was the driving force, she was omitted from the award until a prominent member of the Academy insisted she be included. Marie was thirty-six years old.

> ⇒ **What's the best team you've ever been a part of? What made it great? What can you do to replicate that experience?**

Science was the new frontier, and its pioneers raced toward new discoveries.

Between 1898 and 1902, the Curies published thirty-two scientific papers. In his Nobel acceptance speech, Pierre acknowledged that, placed in "criminal hands," radium was dangerous, but he believed "humanity will derive more good than bad from new discoveries."

On April 19, 1906, Pierre wandered absentmindedly in front of a wagon during a Paris rainstorm, slipping, falling, and dying immediately. For Marie, losing Pierre meant losing "all hope and support."

Marie overcame this obstacle with the determination she exhibited during other setbacks. Three weeks after Pierre's death, the University of Paris physics department offered Pierre's chair to Marie. She accepted, planning to cement Pierre's legacy and, in the process, becoming the university's first female professor.

Returning to her work, Marie balanced speed of discovery with precision as she experimented to isolate radium. The process took her "almost four years to produce the kind of evidence which chemical science demands."

By 1911, Marie was at the center of achievement…and scandal.

She and one of Pierre's former students were discovered having an affair. Though Marie was a widow, Paul Langevin was married—unhappily, but married. Although this scandal provided ammunition for Marie's academic opponents, Marie's growing international reputation prompted the Royal Swedish Academy of Sciences to award her the Nobel Prize in Chemistry. There was one condition: she could not accept the award in person.

Marie Curie refused to back down. In a December 5, 1911, letter to the Academy, she wrote, "there is no connection between my scientific work and the facts of private life." She advised the Academy she would travel to Stockholm.

Her acceptance speech was delivered with dignity, magnanimity to others in the scientific community, and confidence.

> ➡ **You judge yourself by your intentions but judge others by their actions. What would happen if you flipped this perspective?**

Marie Curie died in 1934 at age sixty-six from exposure to radiation, which she and Pierre had discovered.

In 1995, sixty years after her death, the remains of Pierre and Marie Curie were transferred to the Panthéon in Paris, making Marie the first woman to be so honored on her own merits.

Jesse Owens Wins Unprecedented Fourth Gold Medal at Berlin Olympics

How a Vote in America and a Coach's Decision in Berlin Dispelled the Myth of Aryan Supremacy

> "The battles that count aren't the ones for gold medals. The struggles within yourself—the invisible, inevitable battles inside all of us—that's where it's at."
>
> **—JESSE OWENS**

Political storm clouds were swirling.

As the Summer Olympics opened in Berlin on August 1, 1936, before a capacity crowd of one hundred thousand, the skies threatened rain and temperatures hovered around a chilly 64°F (18°C).

Adolf Hitler was using the Olympics as his international stage to display Germany's resurgence; he expected German athletes to demonstrate the concept of Aryan superiority. Hitler's expectations soon would be dashed by Jesse Owens.

By any label—persistence or passion, stubbornness or stamina, drive or determination—Owens, like all great athletes and leaders, demonstrated the will to win. He was motivated to do better.

As an African American born in Alabama in 1913, Owens encountered challenges right out of the starting blocks. He was the youngest of ten children, and when he was nine years old his family moved to Ohio as his father pursued better employment opportunities. Young Jesse delivered groceries, loaded freight, and worked in a shoe repair shop to contribute to the family's income.

He developed a passion for running and became a star on his junior high track team. His performance at the 1933 National High School Championship in the 100-yard dash and long jump tied world records and led to a spot on Ohio State University's track and field team. Forced to work to pay college tuition because he wasn't offered a scholarship, Owens also was required to live off-campus and, on team trips, directed to eat and stay at "blacks only" restaurants and hotels.

In personal and professional battles, the first battle you fight is the one between your ears.

> ➡ How would your characterize your will to win? What about those on your team?

For Owens, competing against America's best athletes brought out his best.

At a college meet in May 1935, Owens astonished the sports

world by setting three world records in the long jump, 220-yard sprint, and low hurdles, and tying a fourth record in the 100-yard dash. All within a span of forty-five minutes.

The following month, Owens and his teammates traveled to California to face formidable competition from the University of Southern California. Owens won the 100-yard dash, 220-yard dash, and 220-yard low hurdles, racking up 40 of Ohio State's 40.2 points. The Buckeyes finished second behind the first-place Trojans. Owens stole the show. He was headed to the Olympics.

Or was he? Before he and America's best amateur athletes could depart, a political hurdle had to be cleared.

In 1931—before Hitler came to power—the International Olympic Committee voted Berlin to host the 1936 games. Hitler's September 15, 1935, Nuremberg Laws declared Jews and others second-class citizens. As the 1936 Games neared, Hitler's anti-Semitic stance prompted America to consider a boycott.

On December 6, 1935, Hitler's representative met with Amateur Athletic Union leaders, giving assurances that Germany would allow blacks and Jews to participate. AAU delegates were locked in a moral conflict. If America boycotted, politics and sports would comingle and deprive athletes who had trained the chance to compete. Sending athletes to Berlin risked signaling America's endorsement of Nazi policies.

On December 9, AAU leaders revealed that in a poll taken of America's Olympic athletes, only one preferred a boycott. By a vote of 58.25 to 55.75, the AAU voted to participate. A different outcome would have meant no Jesse Owens at the Olympics.

Now, Owens and 358 other American athletes were bound for Berlin to compete against the world's best athletes.

➡️ **Who—companies or people, inside or outside your industry—do you measure yourself against to bring out your best?**

Owens competed with racism at home and Nazism in Germany before writing his name in the record books.

On August 3, Owens lined up against five other athletes in the Games' most prestigious event: the 100-meter sprint. A morning rain had softened the red clay track, guaranteeing slower race results. "There were six of us finalists, all with gold-medal ambitions," said Owens, "yet there could be only one winner. I thought of all the years of practice and competition. I saw the finish line, and knew that ten seconds would climax the work of eight years." Owens won with a time of 10.3 seconds, equaling the world record and defeating American Ralph Metcalfe by one tenth of a second and the Netherlands' Tinus Osendarp by two tenths of a second.

The next day, Owens set a world record for the 200-meter sprint and two hours later set another world record in the long jump.

On August 7, Coach Lawson Robertson made a controversial decision, naming Owens and Metcalfe to the 4 × 400-meter relay team. Sam Stoller and Marty Glickman—both Jewish— had expected to run. American sportswriters wondered—likely correctly—if anti-Semitism played a role. "They are likely to criticize any decision I make," said Robertson, "but my job's to put the best possible teams in the race." Yet Owens clearly was the best sprinter. So why had he not originally been placed on the team?

The next day, Jesse Owens led the relay race, Metcalfe stretched the lead, Foy Draper held it, and Frank Wykoff broke the tape with a new world record. Robertson's decision sent Owens into the history books with four gold medals.

We're passionate about sports because we know who wins and who loses. There may be disappointment, but there is no ambiguity.

➡ In your world, where victory's margin can be razor thin and time is money, how speedy is your decision-making? What steps can you take to accelerate your implementation?

You don't need to be as fast as Jesse Owens to win your races. Just focused.

Henry Ford Doubles Workers' Wages

How $5 a Day Changed the World

| "A business that makes nothing but money is a poor business."

—HENRY FORD

Henry Ford may have known his decision would change the business world.

He knew for certain the persistent problems created by his company's unprecedented success required a solution.

Ford was born on a Michigan farm, and his father "thought that I ought to be a farmer," Ford recalled, but it was Ford's mother who taught him the values of work: "Life will give you many unpleasant tasks to do; your duty will be hard and disagreeable and painful to you at times, but you must do it."

Ford was drawn to mechanics, leading childhood projects with other boys to create dams with waterwheels and other mechanical marvels. Everyday chores bored Ford, and he "tried shortcuts" to avoid manual labor; he'd rather "watch a threshing machine work."

His belief in an honest day's work, an obsession with efficiency, and a fascination with mechanics would become central to the Ford Motor Company's success.

When Ford's mother died in childbirth, the twelve-year-old was devastated. But that summer, traveling between Dearborn and Detroit, the wagonload of Fords encountered a steam-powered vehicle. Henry jumped off the wagon, engaging the engineer in conversation. Looking back, Ford figures, "It was that engine which took me into automotive transportation." Four years later, Ford left home and found work in Detroit at James Flowers & Brothers Machine Shop.

In 1891, Ford joined the Edison Illuminating Company and two years later was promoted to chief engineer.

On his own time, Ford invented a self-propelled gas-powered vehicle he test-drove on June 4, 1896.

That August, while attending a conference, Ford secured an invitation to an exclusive dinner where Thomas Edison was the guest of honor. Edison learned that Ford had developed a gas car and invited Ford to join him at the front table, where Ford sketched his invention. "Young man," said Edison, "that's the thing; you have it. Keep at it!"

This conversation initiated a lifelong friendship between Edison and Ford. More important, the encouragement from America's genius inspired Ford to start a company to manufacture his gas-powered vehicle.

➡ **It's the leader's job to bring out the best in people. Who brings out your best?**

Ford's first two companies failed.

In 1899, Ford resigned from Edison, founding the Detroit Automobile Company with funding from Detroit industrialist William Murphy. Ford's passion was pursuing engineering excellence, but any strength overexercised can become a weakness: Ford was unwilling to stop tinkering. The automobiles' quality, he believed, was too low and the price too high. Production stalled. The company dissolved in seventeen months.

Investors continued to back Ford. The former company's assets were transferred into a new company, and Ford developed a racing car. Investors wanted Ford to modify the prototype for public sale, but Ford wasn't interested. The investors hired consultant Henry Leland to appraise the business for liquidation. Leland recommended reorganizing the business to manufacture a single-cylinder automobile similar to one he'd developed for Oldsmobile, using his groundbreaking technique of interchangeable parts. The company wasn't big enough for both men, and Ford left the company within three months in 1902. The Henry Ford Company became the Cadillac Motor Company, and Leland became its president, selling Cadillac to General Motors in 1909.

For Ford, the third time was the charm.

With fearless Barney Oldfield behind the wheel, Ford's race car won the Manufacturer's Challenge Cup in October 1902. Nine months later, the Ford Motor Company was incorporated. Twelve investors, including the Dodge brothers and James Couzens, were among the new company's investors.

By summer of 1903, the first Model A's were being produced, and on July 15—as the company's balance sheet crept toward zero—a Chicago dentist made the first purchase. By August 31, the balance sheet showed $23,000, more than $500,000 in 2018 dollars.

Yet once again, Ford's incessant tweaking threatened the company's survival. Couzens stepped in. Although he knew little about manufacturing, he knew plenty about business, and he urged Ford "to get the cars out and get the money for them, regardless of whether he could improve them."

> ➡ **Great companies share three competencies. Exceptional companies leverage one as their competitive advantage: operational excellence, innovation, and customer intimacy. What's your strongest competency? How can you build on it?**

Henry Ford's vision of manufacturing a light, sturdy, inexpensive car to "meet the needs of the multitude" was realized as the first Model T's rolled out of Ford's factories in early 1909.

Ford couldn't make cars fast enough.

By spring of 1913, Ford Motor Company introduced a revolutionary manufacturing concept: the assembly line, "taking the work to the men instead of the men to the work." By mid-1913, Model T assembly time decreased from 595 man-minutes to 226.

Now there was a new problem. Assembly-line drudgery increased turnover to an astronomical 370 percent annually. Three years earlier, the company's twenty-acre park for Ford employees' families buoyed morale, but turnover persisted. Ford hired John Lee to investigate. Lee's 15 percent "skill-wages classification system" helped but did not solve the problem.

By December 1913, Henry Ford was growing impatient. Sometime between Christmas and New Year's Eve, Ford reached his historic decision.

On New Year's Day in 1914—a Thursday—Ford summoned his top managers. Ford wrote *$2.34 day for a nine-hour day* on a blackboard. "Figure out how much more we can give our men," Ford said. Discussion ensued. Consensus was reached.

On January 5, 1914, the Ford Motor Company astounded the world when it announced it would reduce the workday from nine hours to eight, and double worker pay from $2.50 to $5 a day. "One's own employees ought to be one's own best customers," said Ford.

He was right. Within days, between ten and twelve thousand men applied for jobs at Ford Motor Company. In 1914, 308,000 Model T's were sold—more than all other carmakers combined. In 1915, sales climbed to 501,000. By 1920, Ford was selling a million cars a year.

> ➡ **Are people trying to join your organization or leave it? Are you surprised when good people leave? Who on your team is at risk of leaving, and what should you do about it?**

Henry Ford's decision led directly to the Minimum Wage Fairness Act of 1938, propelled America's twentieth-century prosperity, and created a culture of consumerism that produced the wealthiest nation on Earth.

Acknowledgments

When I finished writing my fourth book, I figured it would be my last.

My wife, Janet, eagerly seconded my decision. And then a couple of years ago, she surprised both of us by wondering aloud if any of the one hundred blogs I'd written in the ensuing three years could be gathered into a new book. My agent, Cynthia Zigmund, sifted through some of my blogs and liked the historical backstories providing context for leadership lessons. Cindy's direction to explore this avenue supported responses I received from executives to my blogs, and her advice and counsel over the years have been invaluable. The idea took shape, and I began researching entries for this book.

Meg Gibbons and her team at Sourcebooks brought this book to life, and Greg Carr and Jeff Travis helped me navigate legal waters. Scholars, historians, journalists, and others who established the facts supporting each of the book's fifty-two vignettes are recognized and recommended in the bibliography.

The men and women leaders I work with around the world inspire me on a regular basis as they accept the weighty responsibility that comes with the territory, and I'm grateful they are willing to share with me their experiences of making decisions.

Elizabeth Bryant, Steve Dalton, Hugh Kennedy, Gordon Leidner, Ray Napolitan, Mike O'Toole, Mark Schortman, and Ashley Sheetz read the manuscript and allowed their names to be associated with this work.

My wife, Janet, and our daughter, Jordan, answered countless questions from beginning to end, and this book reflects their contributions.

Thank you all.

About the Author

Greg Bustin advises leaders at some of the world's most admired companies, and he's dedicated a career to working with CEOs and the leadership teams of hundreds of companies in a range of industries. He's facilitated more than two hundred strategic planning sessions, and he's delivered more than five hundred keynotes and workshops on five continents. This is his fifth leadership book.

Twitter: @GregBustin
Facebook: @GregBustinAccountability
LinkedIn: linkedin.com/in/gregbustin
Email: greg.bustin@bustin.com

Bibliography

PREFACE

Hillaker, Harry. "A Tribute to John R. Boyd." *Code One Magazine*, July 1997. Reposted January 28, 2015. http://www.codeone magazine.com/f16_article.html?item_id=156.

WEEK 1

Kuntz, Tom, ed. *The Titanic Disaster Hearings: The Official Transcripts of the 1912 Senate Investigation.* New York: Pocket Books, 1998.

Loss of the Steamship "Titanic": Report of a Formal Investigation into the Circumstances Attending the Foundering on April 15, 1912, of the British Steamship "Titanic," of Liverpool, after Striking Ice in or near Latitude 41° 46′ N., Longitude 50° 14′ W., North Atlantic Ocean, as Conducted by the British Government. 62nd Cong. (1912).

McCarty, Jennifer Hooper, and Tim Foecke. *What Really Sank the Titanic: New Forensic Discoveries.* New York: Citadel Press, 2009.

WEEK 2

Fant, Kenne. *Alfred Nobel: A Biography.* New York: Arcade Publishing, 1993.

WEEK 3

Caesar, Julius. *Caesar's Commentaries: On the Gallic War and on the Civil War*. Edited by James H. Ford. Translated by W. A. Macdevitt. El Paso, TX: El Paso Norte Press, 2005.

Goldsworthy, Adrian. *Caesar: Life of a Colossus*. New Haven, CT: Yale University Press, 2006.

WEEK 4

A Century of Innovation: The 3M Story. Maplewood, MN: 3M Company, 2002. http://multimedia.3m.com/mws/media /171240O/3m-century-of-innovation-book.pdf.

Huck, Virginia. *Brand of the Tartan: The 3M Story*. Maplewood, MN: 3M Company, 1995.

WEEK 5

Emery, Fred. *Watergate: The Corruption of American Politics and the Fall of Richard Nixon*. New York: Crow Archetype, 2012.

WEEK 6

Weir, Alison. *The Life of Elizabeth I*. New York: Ballantine Books, 1998.

WEEK 7

Speer, Albert. *The Third Reich*. New York: Simon & Schuster, 1970.

WEEK 8

Bennett, Arnold. *How to Live on 24 Hours a Day*. Hyattsville, MD: Shambling Gate Press, 2000.

Gregorian Reform of the Calendar: Proceedings of the Vatican Conference to Commemorate its 400th Anniversary, 1582–1982. Edited by George V. Coyne, Michael A. Hoskin, and Olaf Pedersen. Vatican City: Specola Vaticana, 1983.

WEEK 9

Dunant, Henri. *A Memory of Solferino*. Translated by Mrs. David H. Wright. Philadelphia: The John C. Winston Company, 1911.

Moorehead, Caroline. *Dunant's Dream: War, Switzerland and the History of the Red Cross*. New York: HarperCollins, 1998.

WEEK 10

Donovan, James. *Blood of Heroes: The 13-Day Struggle for the Alamo—and the Sacrifice That Forged a Nation*. New York: Little, Brown and Company, 2012.

Todish, Timothy J., and Terry S. Todish. *Alamo Sourcebook 1836: A Comprehensive Guide to the Alamo and the Texas Revolution*. Fort Worth, TX: Eakin Press, 1998.

WEEK 11

Andrews, Evan. "Remembering the Boston Massacre." History.com, March 5, 2001. http://www.history.com/news/the-boston-massacre-245-years-ago.

McCullough, David. *John Adams*. New York: Simon & Schuster, 2001.

WEEK 12

Alter, Jonathan. *The Defining Moment: FDR's Hundred Days and the Triumph of Hope*. New York: Simon & Schuster, 2006.

Cohen, Adam. "The First 100 Days." *Time*, June 24, 2009. http://content.time.com/time/specials/packages/article/0,28804,1906802_1906838_1906979,00.html.

Smith, Jean Edward. *FDR*. New York: Random House, 2007.

WEEK 13

Current, Richard N. *Lincoln and the First Shot*. Long Grove, IL: Waveland Press, Inc., 1963.

Goodwin, Doris Kearns. *Team of Rivals: The Political Genius of Abraham Lincoln*. New York: Simon & Schuster, 2005.

WEEK 14

Chamberlain, Joshua. *The Passing of the Armies: An Account of the Final Campaign of the Army of the Potomac*. New York: G. P. Putnam's Sons, 1912. https://archive.org/details/passingofarmiesa00cham.

Varon, Elizabeth R. *Appomattox: Victory, Defeat, and the Freedom at the End of the Civil War*. Oxford: Oxford University Press, 2014.

WEEK 15

Kranz, Gene. *Failure Is Not an Option: Mission Control from Mercury to Apollo 13 and Beyond*. New York: Simon & Schuster, 2009.

Lovell, Jim, and Jeffrey Kluger. *Apollo 13*. Boston: Houghton Mifflin Harcourt, 1994.

WEEK 16

Churchill, Randolph S. *The Churchill Documents, Volume 3: Early Years in Politics, 1901–1907*. Hillsdale, MI: Hillsdale College Press, 1969.

Gilbert, Martin. *Churchill: A Life*. New York: Henry Holt and Company, 1991.

Lukacs, John. *Blood, Toil, Tears, and Sweat: The Dire Warning, Churchill's First Speech as Prime Minister*. New York: Basic Books, 2008.

Manchester, William. *The Last Lion: Winston Spencer Churchill: Visions of Glory, 1874–1932*. New York: Bantam Books, 1983.

Manchester, William. *The Last Lion: Winston Spencer Churchill: Alone, 1932–1940*. New York: Bantam Books, 1989.

Norton, Philip. *Eminent Parliamentarians: The Speaker's Lectures*. London: Biteback Publishing, 2012.

WEEK 17

Bowden, Mark. *The Finish: The Killing of Osama bin Laden*. New York: Grove Press, 2013.

Luttrell, Marcus, and Patrick Robinson. *Lone Survivor: The Eyewitness Account of Operation Redwing and the Lost Heroes of SEAL Team 10*. New York: Little, Brown and Company, 2013.

Owen, Mark, and Kevin Maurer. *No Easy Day: The Firsthand Account of the Mission That Killed Osama bin Laden*. New York: Dutton, 2012.

WEEK 18

"How Did the '*Mona Lisa*' End Up in France?" *The Italian Tribune*, March 30, 2016. http://www.italiantribune.com/how-did-the-mona-lisa-end-up-in-france/.

Isaacson, Walter. *Leonardo da Vinci*. New York: Simon & Schuster, 2017.

Sassoon, Donald. *Mona Lisa: The History of the World's Most Famous Painting*. New York: HarperCollins, 2009.

WEEK 19

Hendricks, Nancy. *Senator Hattie Caraway: An Arkansas Legacy*. Charleston, SC: The History Press, 2013.

WEEK 20

Wendt, Lloyd. *The Wall Street Journal: The Story of Dow Jones and the Nation's Business Newspaper*. Skokie, IL: Rand McNally & Company, 1982.

WEEK 21

Jacobs, Charlotte DeCroes. *Jonas Salk: A Life*. Oxford: Oxford University Press, 2015.

Jonas Salk to Max Lauffer, June 2, 1947. Max A. Lauffer Papers. Pitt Faculty, University of Pittsburgh.

WEEK 22

Claridge, Laura. *Emily Post: Daughter of the Gilded Age, Mistress of American Manners*. New York: Random House, 2008.

Perkins, Jeanne. "Emily Post: America's Authority on Etiquette Is a Sensible and Witty Lady Whose Long-Time Best-Seller Is Now Enjoying a Bog Postwar Boom." *Life*, May 6, 1946.

Post, Edwin. *Truly Emily Post*. New York: Funk & Wagnalls Company, 1961.

WEEK 23

Ross, John. *The Forecast for D-Day: And the Weatherman behind Ike's Greatest Gamble*. Guilford, CT: Lyons Press, 2014.

Ryan, Cornelius. *The Longest Day: The Classic Epic of D-Day, June 6, 1944*. New York: Simon & Schuster, 1959.

WEEK 24

Spitz, Bob. *The Beatles: The Biography*. New York: Little, Brown and Company, 2005.

WEEK 25

Browne, Janet. *Charles Darwin: A Biography, Vol. 1—Voyaging*. Reprint edition. Princeton, NJ: Princeton University Press, 1996.

Browne, Janet. *Charles Darwin: A Biography, Vol. 2—The Power of Place*. New York: Alfred A. Knopf, 2003.

Darwin, Charles. *The Autobiography of Charles Darwin*. Revised edition. W. W. Norton & Company, 1993.

Darwin, Charles. *The Foundation of the Origin of Species: Two Essays Written in 1842 and 1844 by Charles Darwin*. Edited by Francis Darwin. Cambridge: Cambridge University Press, 1909.

Quammen, David. *The Reluctant Mr. Darwin*. New York: Atlas Books, 2006.

WEEK 26

Miller, David Humphreys. *Custer's Fall: The Native American Side of the Story*. New York: Meridian, 1992.

Stiles, T.J. *Custer's Trials: A Life on the Frontier of a New America*. New York: Vintage Books, 2015.

WEEK 27

Ellis, Joseph J. *American Creation: Triumphs and Tragedies at the Founding of the Republic*. New York: Alfred A. Knopf, 2007.

Ellis, Joseph J. *Revolutionary Summer: The Birth of American Independence*. New York: Vintage Books, 2013.

Kaufman, Marc. "Jefferson Changed 'Subjects' to 'Citizens' in Declaration of Independence." *Washington Post*, July 3, 2010. http://www .washingtonpost.com/wp-dyn/content/article/2010/07/02 /AR2010070205525.html.

WEEK 28

Taylor, Frederick. *The Berlin Wall: A World Divided, 1961–1989*. New York: HarperCollins, 2007.

WEEK 29

Burl, Aubrey. *Black Barty: The Real Pirate of the Caribbean*. Stroud: Sutton Publishing, 2005.

Johnson, Charles. *A General History of the Robberies & Murders of the Most Notorious Pirates*. London: Conway Maritime Press, 1998.

Sanders, Richard. *If a Pirate I Must Be…: The True Story of "Black Bart," King of the Caribbean Pirates*. New York: Skyhorse Publishing, 2007.

WEEK 30

Whymper, Edward. *Scrambles Amongst the Alps in the Years 1860–1869.* London: J. Murray, 1871.

WEEK 31

Eisenberg, John. *That First Season: How Vince Lombardi Took the Worst Team in the NFL and Set It on the Path to Glory.* New York: Mariner Books, 2009.

WEEK 32

A Brief Narrative of the Case and Trial of John Peter Zenger, Printer of the New York Weekly Journal. Edited by Paul Finkelman. New York: Brandywine Press, 1997.

Kluger, Richard. *Indelible Ink: The Trials of John Peter Zenger and the Birth of America's Free Press.* New York: W. W. Norton & Company, 2016.

WEEK 33

Einstein, David. "Apple Ad Account Up for Bids / Ad Agency BBDO Feels Insulted, Quits." *San Francisco Chronicle*, June 27, 1997. https://www.sfgate.com/business/article/Apple-Ad-Account-Up-for-Bids-Ad-agency-BBDO-2820328.php.

Guglielmo, Connie. "A Steve Jobs Moment That Mattered: Macworld, August 1997." *Forbes*, October 7, 2012. https://www.forbes.com/sites/connieguglielmo/2012/10/07/a-steve-jobs-moment-that-mattered-macworld-august-1997/.

Isaacson, Walter. *Steve Jobs.* New York: Simon & Schuster, 2011.

Siltanen, Rob. "The Real Story Behind Apple's 'Think Different' Campaign." *Forbes*, December 14, 2011. https://www.forbes.com/sites/onmarketing/2011/12/14/the-real-story-behind-apples-think-different-campaign/.

WEEK 34

Smith, Rex Alan. *The Carving of Mount Rushmore*. New York: Abbeville
    Publishing Group, 1985.

WEEK 35

Jones, Clarence B., and Stuart Connelly. *Behind the Dream: The Making
    of the Speech That Transformed a Nation*. New York: St. Martin's
    Press, 2011.

King, Jr., Martin Luther. *Why We Can't Wait*. New York: Signet Classics,
    2000.

WEEK 36

Henry, Ed. *42 Faith: The Rest of the Jackie Robinson Story*. Nashville: W
    Publishing Group, 2017.

Kahn, Roger. *Rickey & Robinson: The True, Untold Story of the Integration
    of Baseball*. New York: Rodale, Inc., 2014.

Lowenfish, Lee. *Branch Rickey: Baseball's Ferocious Gentleman*. Lincoln,
    NE: University of Nebraska Press, 2007.

WEEK 37

McBride, Joseph. *Frank Capra: The Catastrophe of Success*. New York:
    Simon & Schuster, 1992.

WEEK 38

Jones, Dan. *Magna Carta: The Birth of Liberty*. New York: Penguin
    Books, 2015.

WEEK 39

Walker, Dale L. *Mary Edwards Walker: Above and Beyond*. New York:
    Tom Doherty Associates, LLC, 2005.

WEEK 40

Gabler, Neal. *Walt Disney: The Triumph of the American Imagination.*
    New York: Vintage Books, 2006.

WEEK 41

Franklin, Benjamin. *The Autobiography of Benjamin Franklin.* New York:
    Barnes & Noble Books, 1994.

Isaacson, Walter. *Benjamin Franklin: An American Life.* New York: Simon
    & Schuster, 2003.

WEEK 42

Fursenko, Aleksandr, and Timothy Naftali. *One Hell of a Gamble:
    Khrushchev, Castro, and Kennedy, 1958–1964: The Secret
    History of the Cuban Missile Crisis.* New York: W. W. Norton &
    Company, 1997.

Stern, Sheldon M. *The Week the World Stood Still: Inside the Secret Cuban
    Missile Crisis.* Stanford, CA: Stanford University Press, 2005.

WEEK 43

Barker, Juliet. *Agincourt: Henry V and the Battle That Made England.* New
    York: Little, Brown and Company, 2005.

WEEK 44

Alexander, Caroline. *The Endurance: Shackleton's Legendary Antarctic
    Expedition.* New York: Alfred A. Knopf, 1999.

Butler, George, dir. *Shackleton's Antarctic Adventure.* Boston: WGBH
    Educational Foundation and White Mountain Films, 2001.

WEEK 45

Ellis, Joseph J. *His Excellency: George Washington*. New York: Alfred A. Knopf, 2004.

WEEK 46

Lambert, Darwin. *Herbert Hoover's Hideaway: The Story of Camp Hoover on the Rapidan River in Shenandoah National Park*. Luray, VA: Shenandoah Natural History Association, 1971.

Nelson, W. Dale. *The President Is at Camp David*. Syracuse, NY: Syracuse University Press, 1995.

WEEK 47

Frankl, Viktor. *Man's Search for Meaning*. Translated by Ilse Lasch and with a foreword by Harold S. Kusher. Boston: Beacon Press, 2006.

Frankl, Viktor. *Recollections: An Autobiography*. Translated by Joseph and Judith Fabry. New York: Basic Books, 2000.

Redsand, Anna S. *Viktor Frankl: A Life Worth Living*. New York: Clarion Books, 2000.

WEEK 48

Brand, Christo. *Doing Life with Mandela: My Prisoner, My Friend*. London: John Blake Publishing, Ltd., 2014.

Mandela, Nelson. *Long Walk to Freedom: The Autobiography of Nelson Mandela*. New York: Holt, Rinehart and Winston, 1995.

Nelson Mandela Foundation. "Trials and prisons chronology." Accessed September 25, 2018. https://www.nelsonmandela.org/content /page/trials-and-prison-chronology.

WEEK 49

Trimble, Vance H. *Sam Walton: The Inside Story of America's Richest Man.* New York: Dutton, 1990.

Walton, Sam. *Sam Walton: Made in America.* With John Huey. New York: Bantam Books, 1993.

WEEK 50

Curie, Eve. *Madame Curie: A Biography.* New York: Doubleday & Company, Inc., 1937.

Quinn, Susan. *Marie Curie: A Life.* Cambridge, MA: Da Capo Press, 1995.

WEEK 51

Baker, William J. *Jesse Owens: An American Life.* New York: The Free Press, 1986.

Edmondson, Jacqueline. *Jesse Owens: A Biography.* Westport, CT: Greenwood Press, 2007.

Schaap, Jeremy. *Triumph: The Untold Story of Jesse Owens and Hitler's Olympics.* New York: Houghton Mifflin Company, 2007.

WEEK 52

Ford, Henry. *My Life and Work: The Autobiography of Henry Ford.* With Samuel Crowther. Digireads.com, 2011.

Garrett, Garet. *The Wild Wheel.* New York: Pantheon Books, 1952.

Meyer, III, Stephen. *The Five Dollar Day: Labor Management and the Social Contract in the Ford Motor Company, 1908–1921.* Albany, NY: SUNY Press, 1981.

Watts, Steven. *The People's Tycoon: Henry Ford and the American Century.* New York: Vintage Books, 2006.